The

World Wide Web

FOR BUSY PEOPLE

The

World Wide Web

FOR BUSY PEOPLE

Stephen L. Nelson

Osborne/**McGraw-Hill**

Berkeley / New York / St. Louis / San Francisco / Auckland / Bogotá
Hamburg / London / Madrid / Mexico City / Milan / Montreal / New Delhi
Panama City / Paris / São Paulo / Singapore / Sydney / Tokyo / Toronto

Osborne **McGraw-Hill**
2600 Tenth Street
Berkeley, California 94710
U.S.A.

For information on translations or book distributors outside the U.S.A., or to
arrange bulk purchase discounts for sales promotions, premiums, or fundraisers,
please contact Osborne **McGraw-Hill** at the above address.

The World Wide Web for Busy People

234567890 DOC 99876

ISBN 0-07-882244-0

Acquisitions Editor: Joanne Cuthbertson
Project Editor: Janet Walden
Copy Editor: Jan Jue
Proofreader: Pat Mannion
Indexer: David Heiret
Graphic Artists: Lance Ravella, Richard Whitaker
Computer Designers: Roberta Steele, Leslee Bassin, Peter F. Hancik
Quality Control: Joe Scuderi
Series and Cover Designer: Ted Mader Associates
Series Illustrator: Daniel Barbeau

To Elizabeth and Britt-Marie, who enrich my life in ways too numerous to list

About the Author

Stephen L. Nelson, a best-selling author and consultant, has written over 50 books and more than 100 articles on using computers for personal and business financial management. His books have sold over 1 million copies in English and have been translated into 11 different languages.

Contents at a glance

Contents

ACKNOWLEDGMENTS

A book like this is really a group project. Lots of people contribute in all sorts of ways. So I want to thank them here, right up front.

Thank you, Joanne Cuthbertson, acquisitions editor, for conceiving of this book idea, organizing much of the material, and then (most of all) for letting me have the fun of writing it. Thank you, Heidi Poulin, one-time editorial assistant (and now associate project editor), for playing the role of a friendly traffic cop and thereby keeping contracts and chapters flying up and down the West Coast. Thank you, Janet Walden, project editor, for being such a sweet person to work with and for producing a great book in record time. Thank you, Jan Jue, copy editor, for happily addressing the inadequacies of my high school English composition classes. Thank you, Pat Mannion, proofreader, for fixing all the little bugs and gnats—and thereby polishing the prose and pages. Last but not least, a special thank you to the folks in Osborne/McGraw-Hill's production department—Lance Ravella, Richard Whitaker, Leslee Bassin, Roberta Steele, Peter F. Hancik, and Joe Scuderi—you did a wonderful job at laying out the pages of this book.

Steve Nelson
June 14, 1996

INTRODUCTION

The World Wide Web is pretty neat. For once, a new technology really does live up to the hype. But you know what? It's not as easy to use as you might think. Oh sure, there are people who tell you that all you need to do is click a mouse. And that's almost true, I guess. But if you really want to do real work (or have some serious fun), you need to know more than just how to click a hyperlink.

Another problem with the Web—and I'll admit this right up front—is that this baby can waste your time. Lots of your time. So for these two reasons it makes sense for you to invest a bit of effort up front in learning how the Web works, how you can better work with it, and what to do when it won't work.

Why This Book?

The basic premise of this book is simple. You're a busy guy or gal. And you don't want to and can't spend the time required to get the equivalent of a graduate degree in Webology. I hear you. And so does the publisher. This book gives you the low-down on the Web in as expeditious a fashion as it possibly can. Restated in a slightly different way, I respect your time. I know you have other things to do with your life. So this book amounts to a fast-paced (but fun-paced) romp through the information you'll need to become proficient in using the Web as a tool.

I have to tell you one other thing, too. (And I'm not just salving my own ego. Or at least I don't think so.) This book is fundamentally different from the other Web books you'll see on the bookstore shelves. This book treats the Web as a tool you can use for real work and a toy you can use for having or planning serious fun. The other books (and I read all of them as part of doing my research for this book) focus on the technology of the Web. You'll read about all sorts of neat stuff, no doubt. But I figure you don't have time to get into a lengthy discussion of the pros and cons of all of the little nuances and subtleties of the Web. I figure you're a big-picture person.

How This Book Is Organized

The World Wide Web for Busy People provides 14 chapters and three appendixes. You can take a look at the Table of Contents if you're curious about where I stuck stuff. But I do want to mention a handful of quick points about what the different chapters cover. For starters, you should definitely read or at least review the first three chapters. They introduce the big picture, give you a tour of the World Wide Web, and explain the nitty-gritty details.

The most important chapter in this book is Chapter 4. It describes in detail how you use something called a search service to find stuff. If you read nothing else, read this chapter. It should save your hours and hours of time. No kidding.

The Web is pretty much taking over the rest of the Internet, so Chapters 5 and 6 quickly describe the other Internet services you'll encounter after clicking a hyperlink. If you're looking for some way to reduce your reading time, these are the first two chapters I would skip.

Chapters 7, 8, and 9 talk about how to do real work and have real fun with the Web. You may not want to read each of these chapters front to back. (The money management chapter is particularly long, I confess.) But do remember that there's quite a bit of information in these chapters about how you can use the Web for all sorts of cool stuff. Retirement planning. Researching a car purchase. Having a baby. The list goes on.

Chapter 10 provides some trouble-shooting tips. Look here if you get into trouble or you're a compulsive worrier.

Chapter 11 describes how you too can become a web publisher. I'll even show you how to work with HTML. Sort of.

Chapters 12, 13, and 14 itemize, in laundry-list fashion, some of my favorite business, personal, and kid-related web sites. If you're just noodling around or looking for something to do, take a peek at these short chapters.

I also included three appendixes. Appendix A explains how you install web browser software and how you connect to the Internet. Appendix B explains how to browse the Web using Microsoft's Internet

Explorer web browser. Appendix C explains how to browse the Web using Netscape on an Apple Macintosh. (I included Appendixes B and C because the regular chapters of this book emphasize how things work if you're running Netscape on an IBM-compatible PC with Windows 95. Internet Explorer and Mac Netscape users, however, should be able to get up and running easily by replacing Chapter 2 with the appropriate appendix.)

Conventions Used Here

Busy People books use several common conventions. So that you get maximum value from your reading, let me explain them quickly.

Fast Forwards

Each regular chapter begins with a Fast Forward section that summarizes the main points of the chapter. You can use the Fast Forward to preview the chapter's material. If you've already read the chapter or you know the material covered in the chapter, you can also use the Fast Forward to review the chapter's information. (For example, if you were back in school and you were studying for a test, you could probably use the Fast Forwards as a study review.)

Habits & Strategies

You'll find "habits and strategies" marginalia peppering the pages of this book. These amount to little tangential asides where I clue you in to some trick you may want to try or some technique you might want to know about.

Margin Notes

Every so often there's a miscellaneous bit of information that doesn't quite fit into the normal flow of the chapter—but that's still useful. I stuck these blurbs into the margins as "Margin Notes."

Caution

You can't get into too much trouble browsing the Web. Even so, there are a few places where you'll want to be careful. To make these warnings stand out, I placed them in the margin as "Cautions."

Shortcuts

Oops. Almost forgot. I also scattered some quick-and-dirty shortcut ideas around. You'll see these set off as a margin element identified as "Shortcuts."

On From Here

As mentioned earlier, the place to start is Chapter 1. After that, you'll want to proceed to either Chapter 2, Appendix B, or Appendix C, depending on the browser and computer you're using.

Introduction to the Big Picture

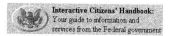

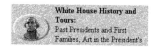

FAST FORWARD

WHAT IS THE INTERNET? ➤ *pp. 4-5*

The *Internet* is a network of networks. In essence, a network is a bunch of computers people have cabled together so that the people who use those computers can share information.

WHAT IS TCP/IP? ➤ *pp. 4-5*

TCP/IP is the networking protocol—think of it as a special language—that the computers of the Internet use to communicate. TCP/IP is what makes the Internet special. It makes the Internet's size, flexibility, and stability possible.

WHAT IS THE WORLD WIDE WEB? ➤ *pp. 5-6*

The *World Wide Web* is a collection of multimedia documents connected with hyperlinks.

WHAT ARE DOCUMENTS? ➤ *p. 5*

A *document* is a written report, a picture, a drawing, a table of financial information—or some combination of these elements. In fact, anything your computer can store in a file can be part of a document, too: sounds, video clips, animation sequences, photographs, and so on.

WHAT IS MULTIMEDIA? ➤ *p. 5*

Multimedia means more than one medium of communication. Text is one medium, but drawings, movie clips, photographs, and music are others. Because World Wide Web documents can use any of these media, people call World Wide Web documents multimedia documents.

What's New:
NPR Customer Service and the
new Federal Election
Commission service

WHAT ARE HYPERLINKS? ➤ *p. 5*

Hyperlinks are pieces of clickable text or clickable pictures. When you click a hyperlink, you tell your computer to display a different multimedia document or to play a multimedia document. (Some multimedia documents are really video clips or sounds.)

WHAT YOU NEED TO GET STARTED ➤ *pp. 6-8*

To get started, you need a computer, a modem, an account with an Internet service provider, and special web browser software. If you can already connect to an online service such as America Online, CompuServe, or the Microsoft Network, you should already have everything you need.

The best place to start, not surprisingly, is at the beginning. So I'll do that here. I want to explain just three things to you: What the Internet (really) is, and what the World Wide Web is, and how you connect your computer to the Internet so you can begin to explore the Internet and its most exciting feature, the World Wide Web. If you've spent more than a few hours browsing the World Wide Web, skip this chapter. You already know what it covers.

WHAT IS THE INTERNET?

You're going to be surprised, probably, to hear me say this, but the Internet itself isn't all that special. All it is, really, is simply a network of networks. That may sound impressive, but once you know that a network is just a bunch of computers some technical geek has cabled together, the big picture comes into focus: The Internet is a bunch of computers—thousands and thousands of them—that are cabled together.

What you may not know, however, is that networks aren't quite as mundane or boring as they sound. By connecting computers, people can easily share information (such as messages and files) and hardware (such as storage disks and printers). You can easily send information to other computers (such as those your friends have at home), for example. And you can easily retrieve information from many of the computers that make up the Internet's networks.

The neat feature of the Internet, therefore, isn't the technology. It's the information: articles on just about any subject, pictures of anything you'd want to look at (and many that you won't want to look at), useful software programs and utilities, and a bunch of other stuff as well.

Oh, I should probably tell you one other thing about the Internet. The networks that make up the Internet all use the same networking *protocol,* or language. (They need to do this so they can communicate, of course.) This common language is called *TCP/IP.* You don't really need to understand anything about TCP/IP, but your computer's operating system needs to know how to talk TCP/IP. Fortunately, TCP/IP protocol is built into Windows 95 and into the newest versions of the Apple Macintosh's operating system, MacOS. For this reason, I strongly recommend you use either a PC running Windows 95 (or later; TCP/IP isn't built into the earlier version of Windows) or a Mac to connect to the Internet. (You can still connect to the Internet using a Windows 3.1 computer, but the lack of built-in TCP/IP makes things more complicated. You have to add extra programs to the operating system so it can "talk the talk and walk the walk.")

WHAT IS THE WORLD WIDE WEB?

The World Wide Web is simply a collection of multimedia documents connected with hyperlinks. You may already know what this means, but let me quickly define these three terms—documents, multimedia, and hyperlinks—to make sure you and I work from a common set of definitions.

A *document* is just, well, a document—such as a written report. You've undoubtedly created hundreds of documents in your lifetime—even if you're still a young person: letters to friends or family, school or business reports, shopping lists, and so on. Most documents you create by hand use words and numbers to communicate their information, but if you use a computer to create a document, you aren't limited to a single medium, or method, of communication. You can create documents (even using a boring old word processor) that use words and numbers, pictures, sounds (such as music), animation, and anything else you can store as a file on a computer. In other words, you can create *multimedia documents*—documents that use multiple media, or methods, of communication.

A *hyperlink* is just a piece of clickable text or a clickable picture in a multimedia document. By clicking a hyperlink with your mouse, you move to another multimedia document. Once there, you'll almost always see other hyperlinks. By clicking these, you can move to still other multimedia documents. Figure 1.1 shows the web page for the White House. As you can see, it contains text and pictures.

What isn't so apparent at first glance is that if you click any of the labeled pictures of the White House's web page, you move to other

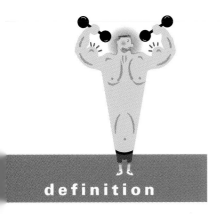

definition

web pages: *The multimedia documents that make up the World Wide Web.*

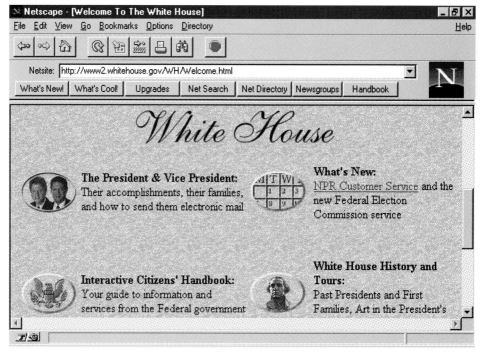

Figure 1.1 The web page for the White House contains hyperlinks to other web pages describing the president and vice president, their families, and the current administration

web pages. For example, if you click the picture of George Washington (shown in the lower-right corner of Figure 1.1), you see the new web page shown in Figure 1.2.

Boiled down to its essence, then, the World Wide Web is just a collection of multimedia documents connected with clickable hyperlinks.

WHAT YOU NEED TO GET STARTED

Despite all of the anxiety-inducing technical mumbo-jumbo you hear about the Internet, you'll find it extremely easy to get started. To begin using the Internet and to view World Wide Web pages, you need only four things.

Figure 1.2 The White House History and Tours web page provides clickable hyperlinks to other web pages

A Computer

You need a computer—either a PC or Mac—it doesn't matter which. Almost certainly, whatever you have will work just fine. (Sure, a new PC or Mac running either Windows 95 or the newest release of the Mac's operating system would be nicest, but I wouldn't give up on the Web if you don't have the latest, greatest hardware.)

If you *are* planning on buying a new computer, or if you have money to upgrade your existing hardware, you should get 16 megabytes or more on your machine. This doesn't directly help you connect to the Web or browse its pages, but more memory makes your PC or Mac do everything faster. So more memory indirectly helps. First and foremost, however, you should get a computer that does well whatever else you want it to do. The Internet stuff is easy.

You may end up saving money by getting the more expensive 28.8 Kbps modem. Using the faster modem, you'll spend far less time connected to your online service.

habits & strategies

If you need a web browser, you can order Netscape's by calling 1-415-254-1900. Microsoft's browser is available from just about any computer store or direct mail business.

A Fast Modem

You need the fastest modem your pocketbook will allow. If you can afford it, for example, get a modem that transmits data at 28.8 Kbps (kilobits per second). You should be able to get a 28.8 Kbps modem for less than a couple hundred dollars. (At that rate, your modem could transmit the text in this paragraph in about a third of a second.)

An Internet Service Provider

You need to sign up with an *Internet service provider,* a company that provides Internet access. There are a bunch of mom-and-pop operations that provide Internet access, but don't waste your time with these. Your best bet here is to use one of the big online services such as America Online, CompuServe, or the Microsoft Network. You'll get better support from any of these online services than from most smaller operations. The larger online services will provide additional content available only to their customers (and that will now include you). And you will have far fewer problems connecting to the service and setting up the software.

I should tell you that others will disagree with me about choosing a big online service as your Internet service provider. Accessing the Internet from one of the mom-and-pop operations often has a certain cachet to it (because it shows, or at least used to show, that you were pretty technically savvy).

A Web Browser

You need to get a *web browser,* which is the software program you'll use to view the web pages. As long as you sign up with one of the big online services as your Internet access provider, you'll get your web browser for free. It will come with the software that the online service provides.

For the figures that appear on the pages of this book, by the way, I used the Netscape Navigator web browser. If you sign up with the Microsoft Network, you'll use Microsoft's Internet Explorer. But it works in the same basic way that Netscape Navigator does.

Appendix B describes how Microsoft's Internet Explorer works, so if you have any questions, you can check there.

ON FROM HERE

I don't want to be too critical of either our hardworking politicians or the evening news media, but I suspect you now know more than most of them do about the Internet. No kidding. But please don't allow your newfound intellectual superiority to stop your learning. There's lots more to learn about both the Internet and, more importantly, about the World Wide Web. The next chapter, for example, provides a hands-on tour of the World Wide Web. And the chapter that follows explains some of the more mysterious technical features of the World Wide Web.

Touring the World Wide Web

FAST FORWARD

STARTING NETSCAPE NAVIGATOR ➤ *pp. 14-15*

To start Netscape, first double-click the Dial-Up Networking shortcut icon and click OK. Then double-click the Netscape Navigator shortcut icon.

WHAT IS A HOME PAGE? ➤ *p. 15*

The first web page you see after you connect to the Internet is your *home page*. Typically your home page resides on the web server provided by your Internet access provider.

MOVING BETWEEN WEB PAGES ➤ *pp. 17-19*

To move between web pages, click a hyperlink. A hyperlink can be a chunk of text or a picture.

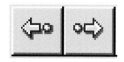

PAGING TO THE PREVIOUS OR NEXT WEB PAGE ➤ *p. 20*

You can page back and forth through the web pages you've already viewed by clicking the Previous and Next buttons.

CREATING AND USING BOOKMARKS ➤ *pp. 21-22*

To tell Netscape it should memorize the current web server or web page address, choose the Bookmarks|Add Bookmark command. To view a bookmarked page, choose it from the Bookmarks menu.

```
Open File...        Ctrl+O
Save as...          Ctrl+S
```

SAVING THE TEXTUAL
PORTION OF A WEB PAGE ➤ *p. 22*

Choose the File|Save As command. Be sure that you use the Save As Type box to specify that you just want "plain text" saved.

```
View this Image (banner.gif)
Save this Image as...
Copy this Image Location
Load this Image
```

SAVING GRAPHIC IMAGES ➤ *p. 23*

1. Right-click the image and choose Save This Image As from the shortcut menu.
2. In the Save As dialog box that appears, use the Save In box to specify in which directory Netscape should save the graphic image file.
3. Use the File Name box to name the file.
4. Then click Save.

I'm going to assume if you're reading this chapter, that it's because you're brand-new to the World Wide Web. And if that's the case, your first experience should really be a quick tour that gives you both a bird's-eye view of the World Wide Web and practical, hands-on experience. So that's what we (you and I) will do here.

STARTING YOUR WEB BROWSER

To begin, you'll need to start your web browser. How you do this depends on which web browser you're using, but if you're using Windows 95 and the Netscape Navigator, you first double-click the Dial-Up Networking shortcut icon, which appears on the Windows 95 desktop:

Windows 95 displays the Connect To dialog box shown in Figure 2.1. If necessary, supply your user name and password. But all the other little bits of data you see in this dialog box should be correct if you've already installed your web browser. (Appendix A describes how you install a web browser.) You got these when you sign up with the Internet service provider. Then click the Connect button. You'll hear your modem dialing the Internet service provider's telephone number, then some beeps and screeching, and then you'll finally be connected.

habits & strategies

If you didn't use the Netscape installation program, you may not see the Dial-Up Networking shortcut icon on your desktop. If so, click the Start button and then choose Programs/ Accessories/Dial-Up Networking. Next, double-click the icon that represents the connection to your Internet service provider.

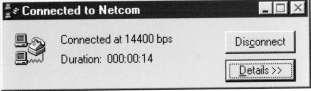

Figure 2.1 You use the Connect To dialog box to supply your user name and password

Once you've successfully made your connection to the Internet, you'll see this small program window:

Note that my connection (made with my ancient laptop) is at 14,400 bps (14.4 Kbps)—a fact which indicates my crying need to bring my laptop up to speed with my desktop machines.

Now, start Netscape by double-clicking the Netscape Navigator shortcut. The Netscape program window appears and loads your first web page, called a *home page* (see Figure 2.2).

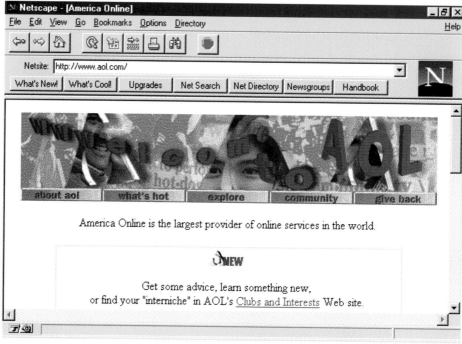

Figure 2.2   The first page your web browser displays is called a home page

YOUR HOME PAGE

The first web page you see after you connect to the Internet is called your home page. Typically your home page resides on the web server provided by your Internet access provider. So, for example, if you're using America Online as your Internet access provider (a good choice, by the way), your home page might look something like the one shown in Figure 2.2. If you're using CompuServe or Microsoft Network as your Internet access provider (two other good choices), your home page will look different. If you've purchased your web browser from Netscape Communications, your web browser may initially use the Netscape corporate web site's home page, too.

If you can't seem to get America Online's web server address entered correctly after a couple of tries, flip ahead to Chapter 3's discussion of URLs.

Before we begin our little tour, there's one thing you need to keep in mind—web page designs change incessantly. So don't expect the web pages shown here to look *identical* to what you see on your screen. Almost surely by the time you take this tour, they will have changed. Note, too, that your display settings may differ from those on the computer used to capture these screen shots.

Now, let's begin. Type the following entry into the Location box. Don't include any spaces. And use periods and not commas in your entry.

www.aol.com

If you have problems, take a look at Figure 2.2. It shows how the Location box (sometimes called a Netsite box depending on the web browser and the web site) looks once you type this string of gibberish. (The gibberish—to which the web browser adds even more gibberish—is called a URL, and it describes a web server's address. But let's postpone a discussion of this complexity until the next chapter.)

USING HYPERLINKS TO MOVE BETWEEN WEB PAGES

The neat thing about the World Wide Web is that if you know how to click your mouse, you can use the Web. As you almost surely know, to click your mouse, you move the mouse (on your desk) so the mouse pointer (which appears on your screen) points to some object on the screen: a chunk of text, a cute little picture, an icon, or whatever. Then you click the mouse's left button. This two-step operation—pointing to some object and then clicking the mouse's left button—is called *clicking* the object.

By clicking on a hyperlink—which can be a chunk of text or a picture—you tell your web browser to move you to another web page. For example, if you click on the About AOL button,

your web browser displays the web page shown in Figure 2.3. Eventually.

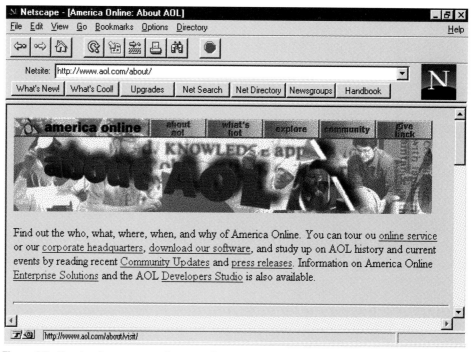

Figure 2.3 Here's what you see after you click the About AOL button

And now you know how to surf the World Wide Web. No kidding. All you have to do is click on a hyperlink. The one thing that can be a little tricky, however, is that hyperlinks don't always stand out on a web page. In Figure 2.3, for example, things are pretty clear. You can probably guess that the buttons across the top of the web page are clickable—and therefore hyperlinks. But take a close look at Figure 2.3. Or better yet, take a close look at your screen if you're following along in front of your computer.

You'll notice that some of the text appears in a different color and is underlined. These colored, underlined chunks of text also represent hyperlinks. So if you click "corporate headquarters,"

corporate headquarters,

your web browser displays the web page shown in Figure 2.4.

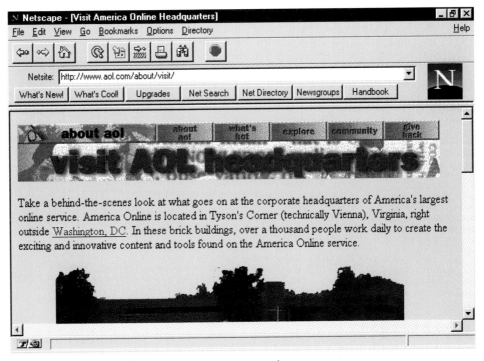

Figure 2.4 This is the AOL corporate headquarters web page

By the way, you've now learned what's really a dirty little secret of the Internet and, in particular, the World Wide Web. It's slow. Even if you've got a superfast modem, you'll spend most of your time waiting for some distant web server to transmit the web page you've requested by clicking a hyperlink.

I don't think, however, that bit of knowledge should make you question your interest in either the Internet or the World Wide Web. The trick is not to waste time waiting for useless information. It's not unreasonable, for example, to spend a few seconds (or even a few minutes) waiting for some really interesting article, a truly unusual photograph, or a handy software utility. What is a waste of time is waiting around for some slick, shallow advertisement that provides no useful content. We'll talk more about this issue—separating the wheat from the chaff—in later chapters of this book.

You don't need to wait until your browser finishes retrieving a web page before you click a hyperlink or page back and forth. You can stop retrieving one page and move to another page at any time.

PAGING TO THE PREVIOUS OR NEXT WEB PAGE

You can page back and forth through the web pages you've already viewed by clicking the Previous and Next buttons.

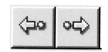

One thing you'll notice if you do this (go ahead and try it right now) is that redisplaying a page you've already viewed takes only a split second.

You can quickly redisplay web pages you've recently viewed because your web browser actually stores, or *caches,* a copy of the web page on your computer's hard disk. So when you redisplay a web page, your web browser only has to grab the file from your hard disk—a very fast operation—rather than grabbing the file from some distant web server.

If you want your web browser to grab a new copy of a web page rather than one from its cache, click the Refresh button.

You might want to do this, for example, if a web page displays information that is constantly updated: web pages linked to cameras that continually take new pictures, weather maps that get updated based on new satellite data, and so forth.

Oh, one other thing. If some web page is taking too long to load, you can always tell Netscape to give up. To do this, click the Stop button.

CREATING AND USING BOOKMARKS

So far, I've purposely avoided a detailed discussion of the painfully cryptic addresses that the Internet uses to identify the precise locations of web sites and their web pages. But one thing you'll quickly find is that this business of clicking your way from one web page to another is time-consuming. For this reason, all of the popular web browsers let you, in effect, memorize the web page addresses. Netscape calls these memorized addresses *bookmarks*.

To tell Netscape it should memorize the current web server or web page address, choose the Bookmarks|Add Bookmark command.

To later view a web page you've marked with a bookmark, choose the Bookmarks|View Bookmarks command. Then, when Netscape displays the View Bookmarks dialog box, choose the web page you want to view from the menu.

Let me explain a couple of other things about the Bookmarks menu shown next. Menu items that show an arrowhead to the right of the menu name display submenus of bookmarks. Netscape organizes the bookmarks in these submenus by category. For example, the Travel menu item displays a submenu of bookmarks for travel-related web pages. Netscape comes with these bookmark categories and their bookmarks already set up, so you can get started exploring the web.

In Netscape version 2.0, you choose the Bookmarks|Go To Bookmarks command.

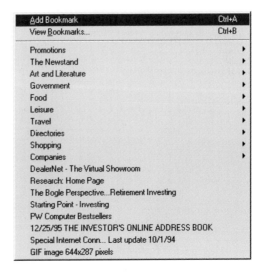

The Bookmarks menu items that don't show arrowheads represent bookmarks the user adds. For example, if you look near the bottom of the menu, you see a menu item entitled The Bogle Perspective: Retirement Investing. In Chapter 7 I write about, among other things, using the Web for retirement planning. I bookmarked the Bogle Perspective web page because I knew I'd want to return there as part of writing that material.

SAVING CONTENT

You can usually save the information shown in the browser window. This means that if some web page shows a picture, you can save the picture. And if some web page has a bunch of text information—maybe it's an interview with Colin Powell that you want to keep—you can save that, too.

Saving the Textual Portion of a Web Page

To save the textual portion of a web page, choose the File|Save As command. When Netscape displays the Save As dialog box (see Figure 2.5), use the Save In box to specify where Netscape should save a file that contains the text portion of the web page. Use the Save As Type box to specify that you just want "plain text" saved. Then use the File Name box to name the text file you're creating. When you finish all this, click Save.

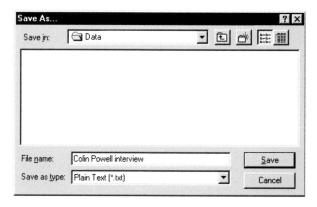

Figure 2.5 Use the Save As dialog box to name the text file and specify where on your hard disk it should be stored

Saving Graphic Images

To save a graphic image shown in a web page, right-click the image so that Netscape displays its shortcut menu. Then choose the Save This Image As command so that Netscape displays the Save As dialog box. Use the Save In box to specify where Netscape should save the graphic image file. Use the File Name box to name the file. Then click Save.

Downloading Files

Some hyperlinks don't point to other web pages. They point to files. When you click one of these hyperlinks, what you're really telling Netscape to do is download, or retrieve, the file from the web server or even another type of server such as an FTP server. I talk about FTP and its special servers in Chapter 6, so let's postpone further discussion of this until then.

FORMS WORK LIKE DIALOG BOXES

You need to know about just one other topic to easily work with the Web: how to use forms. *Forms* are just web pages that include check boxes and option buttons you mark, text boxes you fill in, and command buttons you click. You use forms to order products, play interactive games, register for online services, and enter data for web calculators and search services.

If you know how to work with the dialog boxes displayed when you choose some commands, you know how to work with forms. If you don't know how to do this, you'll need to quickly review how these things work.

Rather than take the time to load a web page that uses each of these form elements, however, let's just take a look at a Netscape dialog box that uses each of these elements. Choose the Options|Preferences command. When Netscape displays the Preferences dialog box (see Figure 2.6), click the Styles tab to display its page of preference settings. (For now, by the way, don't worry about any of these settings. Just focus on the mechanics of using the buttons and boxes that the dialog box displays.)

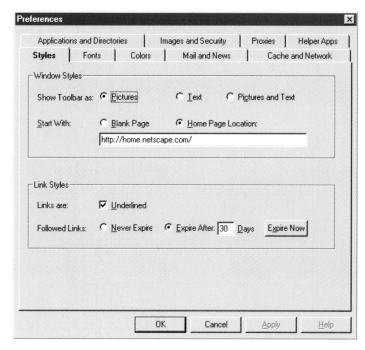

Figure 2.6 This dialog box uses boxes and buttons just as some web page forms do

Along the top edge of the dialog box, in the Window Styles settings, are the Show Toolbar As *option buttons*: Pictures, Text, and Pictures And Text. These option buttons represent mutually exclusive choices for how you want the toolbar—that row of clickable buttons that appears at the top of the Netscape browser window—to appear. You mark your choice by clicking the button. When you click the button, Netscape places a dot,or *bullet,* in the center of the button to show you've selected it. Go ahead and try this if you're not sure how it works. You'll see similar sets of option buttons in many web page forms.

If you look in the Link Styles settings, you'll see a square box with a check mark, labeled Links Are Underlined. This box is called a *check box.* Check boxes, in effect, are on-off buttons. If the check box is marked, Netscape places a check mark or an *X* in the box. To mark and unmark a check box, click the box with your mouse. Again, be sure to try this if you're not clear about how it works. Mechanically, it's not difficult once you realize how check boxes work.

Text boxes represent another element of both dialog boxes and web page forms. In essence, text boxes are simply input blanks you fill in with some bit of information. If you look again at the Link Styles settings in the Preferences dialog box, you'll notice a Days text box. (In Figure 2.6, the value 30 is shown in the text box.) To enter data into a text box, click the box and then begin typing. To replace the contents of a text box, double-click it and then type the new entry.

The final element common to both dialog boxes and web page forms is *command buttons.* You click command buttons to tell Netscape to accept the information you've provided by clicking buttons and filling in boxes. The dialog box in Figure 2.6, for example, has the standard OK, Cancel, and Help command buttons. It also has an Expire Now and an Apply command button. Web page forms don't usually have these command buttons, but you'll often see another command button named something like "Submit," "Search," or "Send." Clicking one of these buttons tells your web browser to send the information you've entered with the form to the web server so it can process the information.

ON FROM HERE

You know what? You now know the basics of using the World Wide Web. Sure, there's lots more to talk about. And, to be quite honest, a bit of additional research on your part will help you better spend your time exploring the Web. But you're really in pretty good shape.

Let me, however, offer a couple of suggestions. If you're going to spend much time working with the Web, take the 20 minutes or so necessary to peruse Chapter 3. It explains a bunch of stuff that will ultimately save you tons of time.

What's more, everybody who's come this far should probably read Chapter 4 to learn how you find content you're interested in.

CHAPTER 3

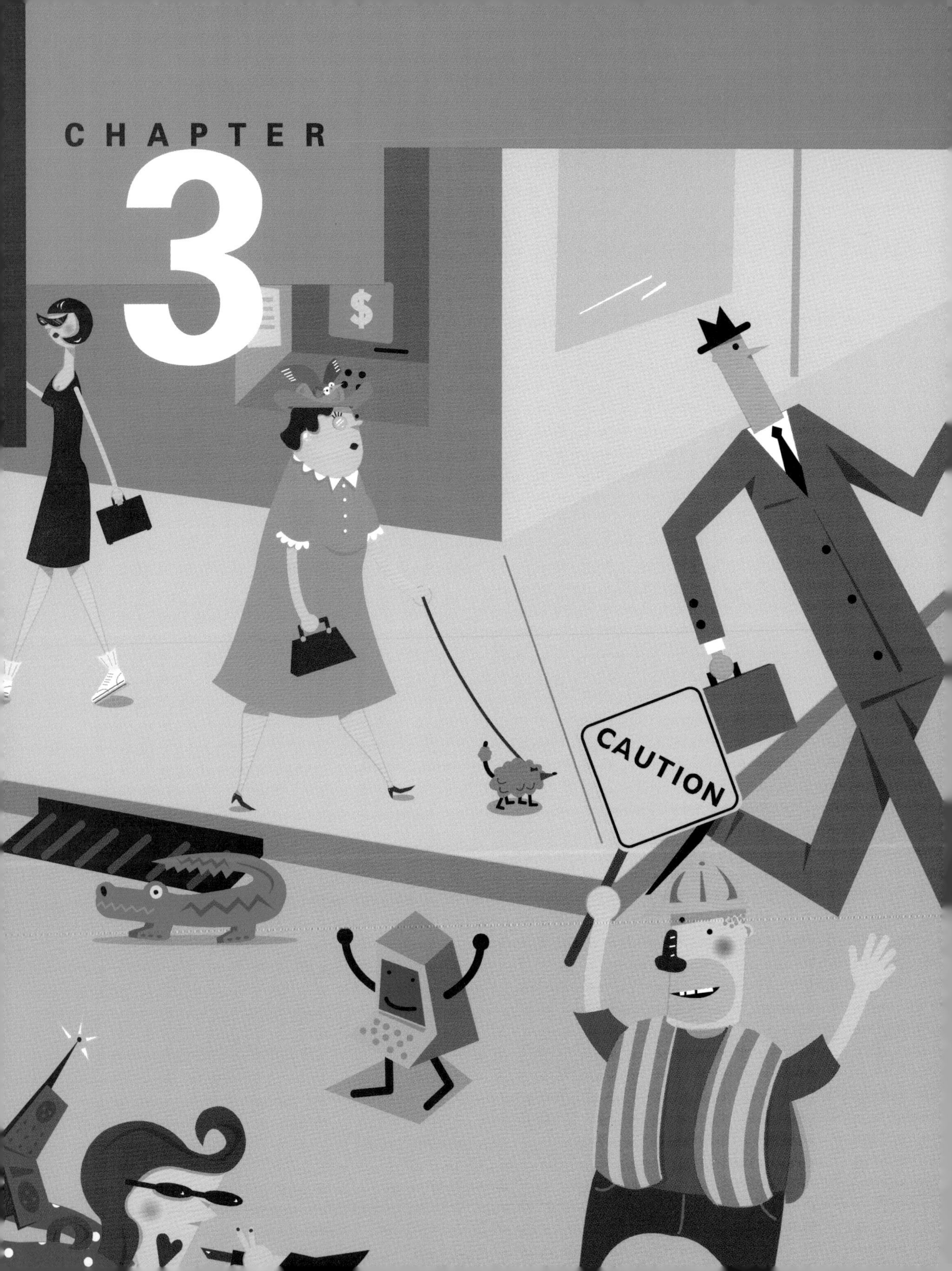

The Nitty-Gritty Details

FAST FORWARD

Location:

11 hours and 59 minutes

Search

Location: ftp://ftp.digital.com/pub/

USING WEB SERVERS ➤ pp. 29-31

Web servers store the web pages you view with your web browser. When you click a hyperlink, your web browser actually requests a web page from a web server someplace.

SECURITY CONSIDERATIONS ➤ p. 31

Web transmissions generally aren't secure; therefore, it's possible to electronically eavesdrop. To remind you about this security risk, Netscape displays a broken key in the lower-left corner of the program window. However, if you have connected to a secure server, Netscape displays an unbroken key.

UNDERSTANDING BANDWIDTH ➤ pp. 31-32

Bandwidth refers to the speed at which data passes through a network connection. Bandwidth is measured in bits per second (bps), kilobits per second (Kbps), or megabits per second (Mbps). Bandwidth, however, often isn't devoted to a single user because the Internet is a packet-switched network.

USING UNIFORM RESOURCE LOCATORS ➤ pp. 33-36

Uniform resource locators (URLs) describe the precise locations of Internet resources such as web servers or web pages residing on web servers. URLs identify the Internet protocol used to provide a particular piece of information, the name of the server, and the name and location of the file.

GOING BEYOND THE WEB ➤ pp. 37-39

Although the Web technically only encompasses web pages (known more precisely as HTML documents), its popularity and ease-of-use means that more and more information resources and Internet services that aren't actually part of the Web are accessible from web pages. For example, you can send an e-mail message, start a Telnet session, or connect to a Gopher or FTP server by clicking a hyperlink.

You make better use of your time and avoid a bunch of common-to-new-user problems if you understand a bit about the mechanics of the World Wide Web. So this chapter gives you a bird's-eye view of the web's architecture. It explains what uniform resource locators (URLs) are. And it defines and discusses most of the technical terms you'll commonly encounter.

This chapter, by the way, isn't supposed to make you some sort of Internet expert. And it's not my attempt to baffle you with jargon. The purpose is to give you some background information to make your exploration of the World Web Wide more interesting, more productive, and more fun.

BIRD'S-EYE VIEW OF WEB ARCHITECTURE

In Chapter 1, I told you that the World Wide Web is composed of multimedia documents, or web pages, connected with hyperlinks. In Chapter 2—if you actively took the tour that chapter describes—you even used a few of these hyperlinks to jump from web page to web page. You know all of this, right? Good.

Web Servers Dish Out Web Pages

Okay. The next thing you need to understand—and probably already intuitively know—is that these web pages are stored on computers someplace. These other computers are called *web sites,* or more accurately, *web servers.* (Some web servers store pages for multiple web sites.)

When you browse the World Wide Web, you actually use two software programs—the web browser, or client, that runs on your computer, and the web server software that runs on the web server. The web *client* requests web pages from the server and displays them on your computer. The web *server* stores web pages and responds to

**habits &
strategies**

If you want to try connecting

to another web server,

try an easy-to-connect-to web

server like Microsoft's World

Wide Web site at

http://www.microsoft.com *or*

Netscape's World Wide Web

site at **http://www.netscape.com.**

requests from the client. The World Wide Web, then, uses what's called *client-server computing*. That means two (or more) computers work together to do what you want.

All of this may seem irrelevant to your web experience, but it turns out to be very relevant. When you can't complete some web task, you'll typically be able to figure out what the problem is (or at least where the problem is) by understanding the nature of the web's architecture.

For example, if you can't connect to any web server—and you've tried several—you can be pretty sure the problem is on your end of the connection. By contrast, if you can connect to another, different web server, you'll know that the client end of the connection works and that the web server is the problem.

If you can connect to some web servers but not the one you want —and you've been able to connect to the web server before—maybe the web server isn't running. Perhaps whoever operates the web server is performing some sort of routine maintenance on the web server. Or maybe the web server is just so darn busy that either the web browser client has given up trying to retrieve a web page from the server, or the web server is so overworked that it isn't taking any additional client requests. In these situations, you can often try connecting again a few seconds or a few minutes later—and usually this works. Or you can simply attempt to connect at some other time of day. (For example, web servers with web pages of interest to teenagers usually get busy after school and after the dinner hour.)

Let me make a couple more minor points. Netscape knows whether a web server uses the Netscape server software. If the server does, some versions of Netscape name the box into which you type the URL the Netsite box. Otherwise, they name it the Location box. (If you're using Netscape version 2.0 or later, the Netsite/Location box doesn't change names.)

| Location: | http://www.microsoft.com/products/ |

Whether a web server uses Netscape's server software or somebody else's probably makes no difference to you, but it may be confusing to see this box's name change when you view some new web page. So

I wanted to mention this kookiness. In the pages that follow, I'm just going to call this thing the Location box.

One other thing I want to say: It's possible that information you enter into a web page form and then send is visible to technically proficient miscreants electronically eavesdropping on your transmission. To deal with this remote possibility, some web browsers and servers secure transmissions by first encrypting information they pass back and forth. Now, most of the time this encryption isn't happening. And to remind you of this, Netscape displays a broken-key icon in the lower-left corner of its program window:

But you should be aware that it's possible someone is monitoring your transmissions, just waiting for the chance to learn your credit card number or some other secret. I don't worry about this kind of stuff. As far as someone illegally charging a trip to Bermuda on my credit card, I figure that's the bank's problem. They are the ones who will pay. And I don't have any super-secret information to transmit over the web inasmuch as I'm not currently involved in any large-scale conspiracy or international intrigue.

Some people, however, aren't quite as nonchalant. So increasing numbers of web servers are secure. (Servers that take credit card orders, for example, often are secure.) When a server is secure, Netscape displays an unbroken key in the lower-left corner of the program window:

If you're connected to a web server that provides the highest level of security, the key shows two teeth. Otherwise, it shows only one.

Bandwidth Matters

Another topic you'll find helpful to understand is bandwidth. What bandwidth really refers to—at least when you're talking about the Internet, networks, and the World Wide Web—is the amount of data a computer can push through a connection.

If you think about the cables that connect the Internet's networks as being like plumbing, bandwidth is pretty easy to understand. You push more water through a bigger pipe. And you push less water through a smaller pipe. So a water pipe that's 4 inches in diameter, say, can move a lot more water than one that's only 1 inch in diameter.

Network bandwidths work in the same, basic way, but people measure network bandwidth in bits per second (bps). The greater the bits per second a modem or network cable can handle, the faster you can move information.

The weird part of bandwidth, however, is that it often isn't all that relevant when it comes to the transmission speed you'll experience. Why? Because the Internet employs what's called *packet-switched networking.* With a packet-switched network, your transmission is broken down into little chunks, called *packets,* and then these individual packets are pumped out into the high-bandwidth cables—essentially big pipes that connect the Internet's networks. As soon as this happens, your packets get all mixed up with other people's packets. This isn't actually a problem: When your transmission's packets reach their destination, the computer at the other end of the connection reassembles the packets.

But—and this is the part you should understand—a packet-switched network means you share bandwidth with everyone else who's transmitting packets over the same part of the network. The fewer people using the Internet, therefore, the faster your transmission times. And the more people using the Internet, the slower your transmission times.

Packets make it difficult to compare bandwidths in a meaningful way. Your modem, for example, might transmit data at 28.8 kilobits per second (Kbps). And that sounds pretty good until you hear about people's T1 connections that transmit data at 1.5 megabits per second (Mbps). The problem is that you actually can't compare these bandwidths unless each is only used by a single user. With a packet-switched network—which is what the Internet is, remember—someone using a 28.8 Kbps modem may be transmitting data almost twice as fast as someone else using one-hundredth (or roughly 15 Kbps of the bandwidth) of a T1 line. Yet you'll encounter people who wax poetically about the speed of the half-share of a T1 line they use along with 50 other, heavy users. When you hear this, just smile smugly. What they don't understand—and perhaps never will—is that the Internet is a packet-switched network.

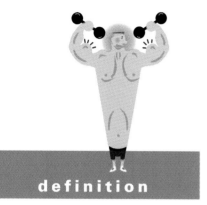

definition

Bit: *A bit is just a single binary digit—either a 1 or a 0. A kilobit is 1,024 bits, by the way. And a megabit is 1,048,576 bits.*

UNDERSTANDING UNIFORM RESOURCE LOCATORS

You've already encountered uniform resource locators if you've read the previous chapter or browsed the World Wide Web even a little bit. The *uniform resource locator (URL),* is the address of a web server or of a web page, and it appears in the Location box at the top of the Netscape window (see Figure 3.1).

The URL, or address, has three parts. The *http://,* which stands for *hypertext transfer protocol,* just identifies what follows as a World Wide Web server or page. This doesn't make sense until you know that the World Wide Web is just one of the protocols that the Internet provides. (I'm going to talk a bit more about this in a minute.)

The second part of a URL names the web server. Typically this part starts with the three letters *www* and then is followed by the name of the domain, or computer network, of which the web server is a part.

Figure 3.1 The Location box, near the top of the Netscape window, shows the uniform resource locator for the web page you're currently viewing

CAUTION

A URL never ends with a period, so if you see a URL in this book (or anywhere else) that looks like it ends with a period, don't include it! The period is only there to punctuate the sentence.

SHORTCUT

If you know a web page's URL, you can type it directly into the Location box. What's more, while you can start the URL with http://, you don't have to. If you leave it out, Netscape adds it for you.

For example, in Figure 3.1, which shows the Microsoft web server's home page, the web server's name is *www.microsoft.com,* which means the domain name is *microsoft.com.*

You can identify the type of organization that operates a domain by looking at the domain suffix. The *com* suffix indicates the domain is a commercial network operated by a business. The *gov* suffix indicates the domain is operated by the government network. The *edu* suffix indicates that the domain is operated by a school or university. The *mil* suffix indicates the domain is operated by the military. The *org* suffix indicates the domain is operated by a nonprofit organization. Finally, the *net* suffix generally indicates the domain is operated by an administrative network connecting other networks. (These are just general rules—and you can find exceptions to most of them—but they do give you an idea about who operates a particular web server.)

The last part of the URL names the actual web page and identifies its location on the web server. In Figure 3.2, for example, the web page location and name is */Misc/FAQ.htm.* The */Misc/* part provides the web server directory holding the web page. The *FAQ.htm* part names the web page. By the way, if you don't specify a web page in your URL, the web server typically loads the default web page for that web site, which is often referred to as a *home page.* (This page is frequently named index.htm or welcome.htm.)

Web page names always end either in *html* or *htm. HTML* stands for *hypertext markup language.* HTML is what people use to create web pages.

Now that you know a thing or two about URLs, I can give you a trick for easily remembering them. Take a look at the following URLs, which I gleaned from a couple of car magazines I was reading last night:

```
http://www.jaguarcars.com
http://www.lincolncars.com
http://www.toyota.com
```

Do you see the repetition? They all start the same way—with *http://www.* And they also all end the same way—with the *com* domain name suffix—because these are all commercial web servers. So really, all you need to remember when you see a URL that you want to

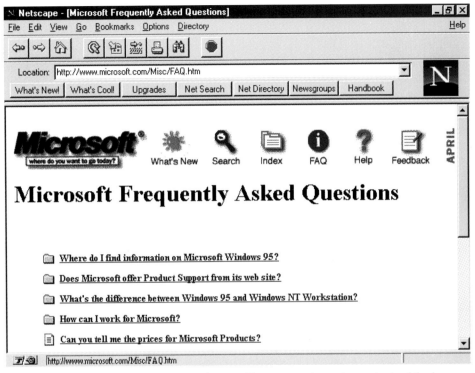

Figure 3.2 When you move to a new web page, Netscape updates the contents of the Location box to show the new page's uniform resource locator

remember or later visit is the part of the URL that's between the *http://www.* part and the *.com* part. Easy, right?

Once you know how URLs are constructed, you can often guess what the URL for a site is. For example, if you wanted to browse the General Motors' web server, you might be able to guess that the web server's URL is **http://www.gm.com/**. And if you wanted to browse Honda's web server, you might correctly guess that the web server's URL is **http://www.honda.com/**.

I should tell you, however, that my method isn't exactly foolproof. As I noted earlier, only commercial web servers use the *com* suffix. So if you're looking for a nonprofit organization's web site, or a government, military, or education site, you swap the *com* suffix with *org*, *gov*, *mil*, or *edu*, respectively.

Another thing that can foul you up is that some *web publishers* (the people who create and name web sites) apparently feel duty-bound to make it more difficult for you to find their sites. (My experience is that the state government sites are this way.) So if you want to view the State of Montana's travel information web server, you use **http://travel.mt.gov/** as the URL, as shown in Figure 3.3.

And even more obtuse, if you want to view the State of California's travel information web site, you use **http://gocalif.ca.gov/** as the URL, as shown in Figure 3.4. By the way, take a look at the URL for the web page shown in Figure 3.4. See that number that follows the web server name? That's called a *port number*. You don't need to enter it. You don't need to worry about it. (In fact, why Netscape even displays it is a mystery to me.)

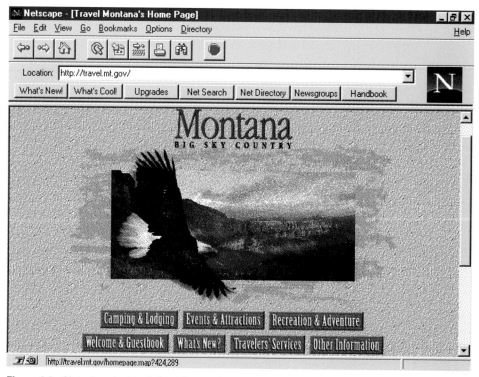

Figure 3.3 Not all web sites follow the naming conventions, as the State of Montana's web site shows

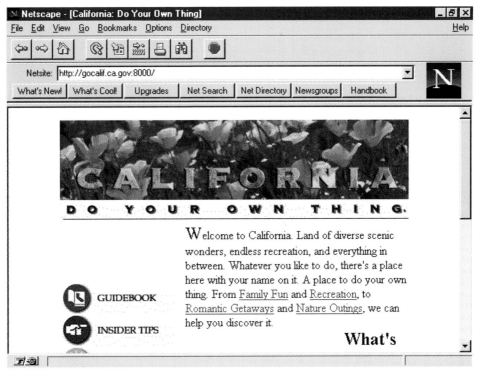

Figure 3.4 Some URLs include a port number, but you don't need to worry about port numbers

THE WEB IS GROWING

While the World Wide Web is really only this large set of multi-media, or HTML, documents, it makes more sense to think of the web as all the information you can view or get to by using a web browser. This is technically inaccurate, but as a practical matter, the cleverness of the web's basic architecture—clickable connections—means that more and more of the Internet's content is available through your web browser.

For example, another feature of the Internet is FTP. *FTP,* which stands for *file transfer protocol,* is completely different from the World Wide Web. FTP moves files between computers. But some of the web page hyperlinks you click will actually lead not to web pages but to FTP sites. An FTP site provides files you can download, or retrieve, for free. Figure 3.5 shows how the web browser window looks when you view

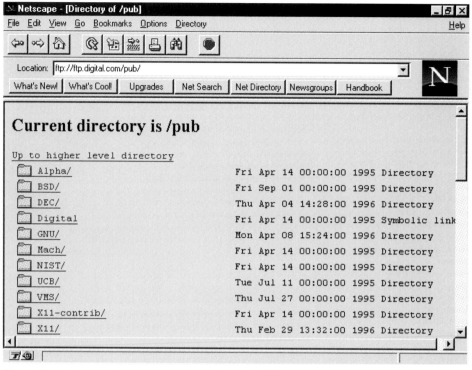

Figure 3.5 Using a web browser, you can also view FTP sites

the contents of this FTP site. Note, too, that the FTP site's URL looks different. It doesn't start with the *http://* prefix because it's not a web page; it starts with the *ftp://* prefix.

Other hyperlinks will lead you to Gopher servers, start Telnet connections, or start an e-mail program you can use to send someone an electronic mail *(e-mail)* message. What's more, both of the most popular web browsers—Netscape Navigator and Internet Explorer— also let you view newsgroups, which is another feature of the Internet.

It makes sense to consider all of this other stuff part of the "web," too. So that's the way I'm going to talk in this book. My basic rule will be this: If you can view it with your web browser, it's part of the Web, and we should talk about it—especially if there's interesting or valuable content provided by the feature. So we'll talk in Chapter 5 about e-mail, mailing lists, and newsgroups and in Chapter 6 about FTP, Gopher, and Telnet.

I'll even make a prediction: The Web will absorb the Internet's other features in the next two years. Very quickly, as a result, the terms *World Wide Web* and *Internet* will become synonymous.

ON FROM HERE

If you've been with me since Chapter 1, you actually know quite a bit about the Internet and the Web. More than most of your friends, I bet. But you still don't know what's probably the most important thing to know: how to find good stuff. So that's what the next chapter describes. If you read nothing else in this little book, take the time to carefully peruse Chapter 4.

Finding the Needle in a Haystack

FAST FORWARD

USING WEB SEARCH SERVICES ➤ *pp. 43-50*

There are two basic means of searching the web: using a directory, or using an index.

SEARCHING WITH WEB DIRECTORIES ➤ *pp. 43-44*

Web directories work like yellow pages directories: you pick a particular category or subcategory, and then look through the entries within that category or subcategory. To use a web directory, you just click hyperlinks.

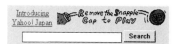

SEARCHING WITH A WEB INDEX ➤ *pp. 44-47*

To search an index, you enter the term or terms you're looking for in the text box provided by the search form. The search service then displays a list of the web pages in its index that use your search terms. Search services all work in roughly the same way, but there are major differences in the quality, depth, and breadth of their indexes.

REFINING YOUR WEB INDEX SEARCH ➤ *pp. 47-49*

You can fine-tune your web index search by providing more detailed instructions to the web search service. Which search options you have, of course, depends on the search service. You can specify searching not just the World Wide Web, but also Usenet newsgroups and e-mail addresses. And you can search using multiple search terms (or *keywords,* as they're sometimes called).

Sure, the Web is neat. But if you've fooled around with the Web for more than a few minutes, you know that it's really tough to find good content. Looking for what you want or for something that's really interesting is like trying to find a needle in a haystack.

Fortunately, the Web does provide tools for locating content—its search services. In this chapter, I'll briefly explain how these search services work, describe in detail how you use them, and finally tell you what to do when they don't work.

USING A WEB SEARCH SERVICE

There are two basic means of searching the web: using a directory, or using an index. I'll quickly describe both techniques.

Using a Web Directory

In essence, the directories work like yellow pages directories: you pick a particular category or subcategory, and then look through the entries within that category or subcategory. For example, suppose you're considering a trip to France and want to see if the web provides any information useful for planning your trip. To begin this search, you could visit the **http://www.yahoo.com** web server, which maintains a directory of other web servers and pages (see Figure 4.1).

At the top of the web page is a search form (I'll describe how this works in just a minute), but if you page down, you get to a directory of web servers. If you click the Travel hyperlink, which is under the Recreation category, you see another web page.

- **Recreation**
  Sports [Xtra!], Games, Travel, Autos, ...

To continue your search, click the hyperlink that best describes the category within which you want to continue the search. If you were really looking for travel information on France, for example, you might click the Regional hyperlink to get to another web page that asks

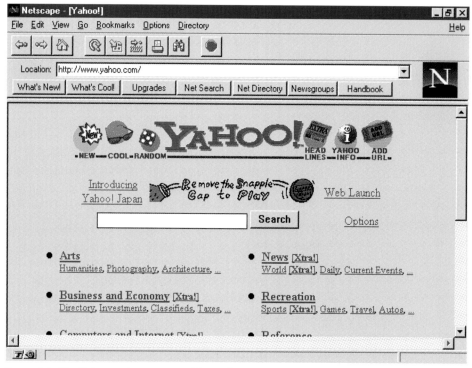

Figure 4.1 The Yahoo web server provides a directory of other web servers and pages

which region you're interested in (see Figure 4.2). After clicking a couple more hyperlinks, you would ultimately get to the web page shown in Figure 4.3.

Web directories are useful. And if you're looking for some bit of information that people are generally interested in—like travel information—you'll find them to be a great aid. But they aren't a panacea. Anytime you want information that doesn't fit neatly into some category, you'll find it very difficult to locate useful data. And that's where the web index comes in.

Using a Web Index

The popular search services—such as Yahoo—have special programs, called *web spiders* or *web crawlers,* that create indexes of the content the spiders find in web pages. When you can't find information using a directory, you can search one of these indexes.

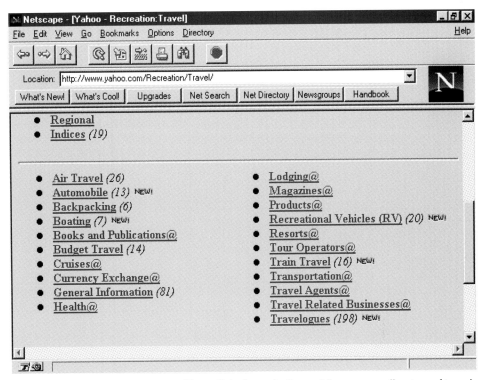

Figure 4.2 After clicking the Travel hyperlink shown in Figure 4.1, you see a directory of travel-related subdirectories

The search forms provided by other search service web sites look very similar to the Yahoo web site.

To search an index, you enter the term or terms you're looking for in the text box provided by the search form. For example, if you're interested in finding a villa in Provence, you might enter the two terms **villa** and **Provence** into the text box. Figure 4.4 shows the search form provided by the Yahoo web site.

Next, use the Search option buttons to indicate whether you want to search the entire search service's index or only that portion of the index that relates to a particular directory category.

After you specify your search terms, click the Search button to begin your search. If the search service finds index entries—either web sites or web pages—that use the term or terms you specify, it displays a web page listing hyperlinks for these pages (see Figure 4.5). To view one of these web pages, click its hyperlink.

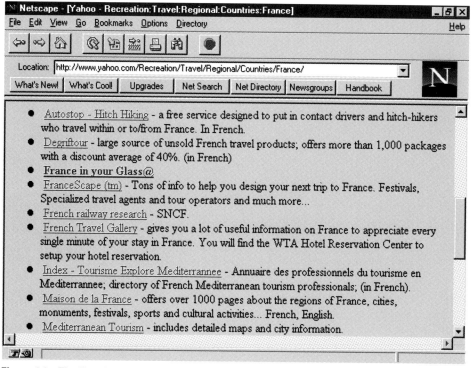

Figure 4.3 The list of web sites providing travelers with information about France

If you find a search service you especially like, take the time to learn it well. I'm giving you just an overview here. There's more to learn about many of these search services— particularly the powerful ones like Alta Vista. (See the next section.)

Here's how a web spider builds its list of web pages that match your search terms. In essence, the web spider goes out and finds web sites or pages that use your search terms. Then it displays a list of the web pages that use your terms, placing the pages that use the terms the most at the top of the list. This simple approach generally works pretty well, but it can produce undesirable results. For example, you might want to find a web page that describes retirement planning but miss a really good web page that uses this term only one or two times. (You can largely mitigate this problem by looking at all the web pages a search returns and attempting additional searches that use synonym terms.)

You'll also find that some *web publishers*—the people who create web pages—create web pages that purposely use and sometimes inappropriately insert hidden terms (so the text doesn't appear on the web page) that people commonly search on. A while back, for example,

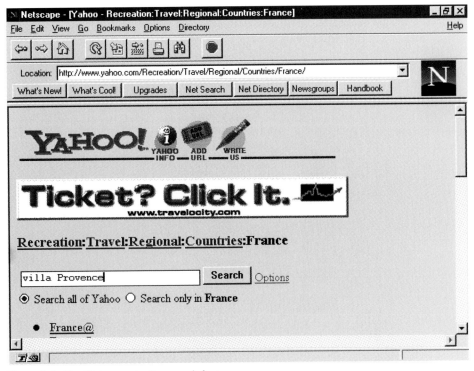

Figure 4.4 The Yahoo web site search form

some computer science student created a web page that simply used the word "sex" about a thousand times (and several other related expressions as well). The only real content of this web page, however, was his resume. I doubt this kid actually found a job this way. But I'm sure a lot of people inadvertently visited his web site. You, of course, may not care about the sex-crazed fools who found this kid's resume. But if you start thinking about some advertiser doing the same thing— and thereby misdirecting your search for, say, investment or medical information—it's quite a bit more irritating.

Fine-Tuning a Web Search

You can fine-tune your web index search by providing more detailed instructions to the web search service. Which search options you have, of course, depends on the search service. But those provided by the Yahoo search service are representative, so let me briefly

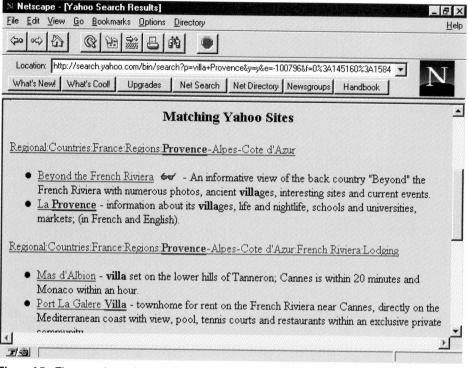

Figure 4.5 The search service will display a web page that provides hyperlinks for the web sites or pages that use your search term or terms

describe those here. If you click the Options hyperlink, which appears next to the Search command button, your web browser displays another web page—only this one provides several additional boxes and buttons that you use to specify the manner in which the search service should work (see Figure 4.6).

Use the Search option buttons—Yahoo, Usenet, or Email Addresses—to describe whether Yahoo should search the World Wide Web, the Usenet newsgroups (collections of e-mail messages organized by category), or a list of e-mail addresses.

The Find Matches That Contain option buttons let you specify what happens when you search using two terms—for example, *France* and *travel*. If you only want to find web pages that use both terms—the typical case—mark the All Keys option button. If you want to find web pages that use either term, mark the At Least One Of The Keys option button.

Chapter 5 describes both e-mail and newsgroups in more detail.

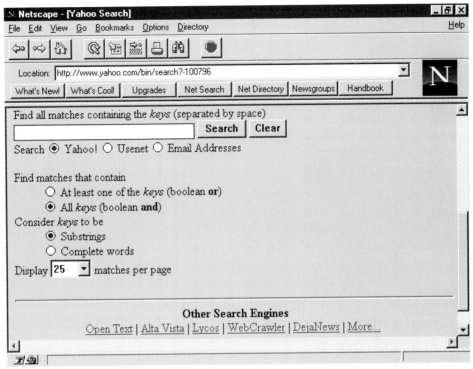

Figure 4.6   The Yahoo search form with the search option buttons and boxes showing

The Consider Keys To Be option buttons let you specify whether your search terms need to be whole words or can be pieces of other words. If you want to find whole words, of course, mark the Complete Words option button—for example, you're searching for the term "villa" and you only want to find this word, not words that use the string "villa" such as "village." Otherwise, mark the Substrings option button.

The Display Matches Per Page text box describes how many web page matches Yahoo should display on one page at a time. (A match occurs when a search term matches a word in the web page.) The default Display Matches Per Page setting is 25, which means that Yahoo attempts to display web page matches in batches of 25. (If Yahoo finds more than 25 web page matches, you can display the next page, or batch, of 25 matches by clicking a hyperlink.)

The Trouble with Search Services

If you've just perused my discussion of web search services, you're probably all excited about how they work and about how much time they'll save you. While I don't want to dampen your enthusiasm, they're not as useful as you might think.

For one thing, the directory portions of a web search service are built pretty much on a do-it-yourself basis. If you create your own web site and want it added to a search service, for example, you submit your directory listing to the search service. You decide (or suggest) the directory category into which the web site should be placed. Maybe that sounds fine. But recognize that you probably categorize information in a slightly different way than I do. And we both probably categorize information differently than the guy or gal down the street. So it's not always easy to find what you're looking for—even if the web site is included in the search service's directory. What's more, there are plenty of good, interesting sites that aren't included in search service directories (perhaps because they're brand-new or the web site operator doesn't know or want to publicize the site).

The indexes can also be problematic. For example, the web spiders don't necessarily update their indexes for changes in a web page's content after the web page has already been indexed once. And it takes a while for new web sites to have their pages indexed, because a web spider finds a new web page by following hyperlinks to the page. Therefore, until a new web page is popularized and has lots of hyperlinks pointing to it, it's pretty hard for the web spiders to find it.

REVIEWING THE POPULAR SEARCH SERVICES

Yahoo isn't the only search service you should know about. There are more than a dozen others and some of them—such as Alta Vista— are better than Yahoo. I'm not going to give you the blow-by-blow account of how you use each of these other services. But it does make sense for you to know what's available and how the various search services differ. (Remember that you don't need to include the *http://* prefix if you're using Netscape or Microsoft Explorer. These browsers, and some others, are smart enough to add the missing prefix if you leave it out.)

Using Alta Vista

Digital Equipment Corporation, which makes fast microcomputers and even faster big computers, provides the Alta Vista search service. Alta Vista offers a huge index both of web sites and Usenet newsgroups. To use the Alta Vista web search service, type the following into the Location text box: **http://altavista.digital.com**. When Netscape displays the Alta Vista search form, use its text box to provide your search terms, as shown in Figure 4.7.

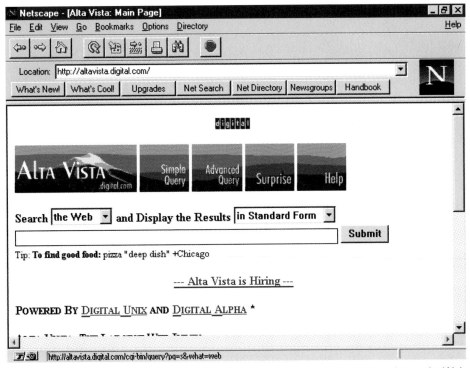

Figure 4.7   The Alta Vista search service is perhaps the most powerful search service on the Web

I like the Alta Vista search service for a bunch of reasons. For one thing, it lets you easily enter a phrase. All you do is enclose the phrase in quotation marks. For example, if you want to search for web documents that use the phrase "University of Washington," you fill in the search form as shown in the following illustration:

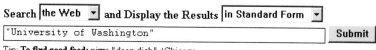

Search |the Web ▾| and Display the Results |in Standard Form ▾|

| "University of Washington" | Submit |

Tip: **To find good food:** pizza "deep dish" +Chicago

By contrast, if you use the search argument "University of Washington" with the Yahoo search service, you won't just get web pages that use the phrase "University of Washington." You'll get any web pages that use the three words "University," "of," and "Washington." Almost every web page, of course, uses the preposition "of." And a bunch of web sites also use the words "University" and "Washington," including those web pages for Washington State University, Washington University, Central Washington University, and so on.

Alta Vista allows you to be much more precise in specifying your search terms by using Boolean operators in your search. Using Boolean logic operators, for example, you can specify that you want to find web pages that talk about Alfonse D'Amato, the senator from New York, but not about the Whitewater senate hearing he chaired, as shown next.

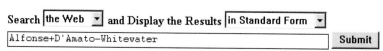

Search |the Web ▾| and Display the Results |in Standard Form ▾|

| Alfonse+D'Amato-Whitewater | Submit |

Tip: **To find good food:** pizza "deep dish" +Chicago

USING EXCITE FOR CONCEPT-BASED SEARCHES

The Excite search service at **http://www.excite.com** lets you search the Web using not only search terms, or what it calls *keywords*, but also by searching for concepts (see Figure 4.8). In addition, you can read reviews of more than 50,000 web pages. I never have much luck with the Excite search service, but some people really like it. So you might as well try it at least once.

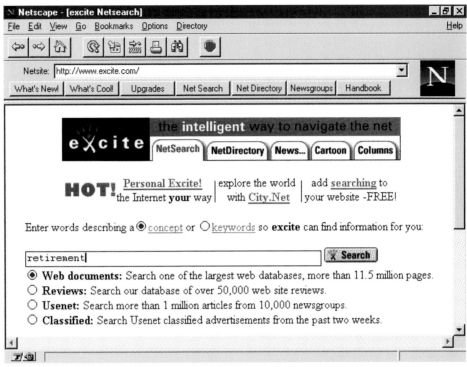

Figure 4.8 The Excite search service indexes search terms (keywords) and concepts

habits &
strategies

With Infoseek, you need to

leave a space between search

terms. For an example, see the

Search for Information About

box in Figure 4.9 .

Using the Infoseek Search Service

Infoseek at **http://www.infoseek.com** is one of the best search services. Some people even think it is the best (although I actually like Alta Vista better). There aren't many tricks to using Infoseek. Correctly capitalize proper nouns. Enclose phrases in quotation marks (as you do with the Alta Vista search service). Precede words or phrases that must appear in a web page with the + character, and words or phrases that must not appear in a web page with the - character. Figure 4.9 shows the Infoseek search form completed to find web pages that use the search terms *D'Amato* and *ethics,* but not *Whitewater.* You might enter such a search argument if you were looking for information about the ethics investigations into Senator D'Amato rather than his investigations into the Whitewater affair.

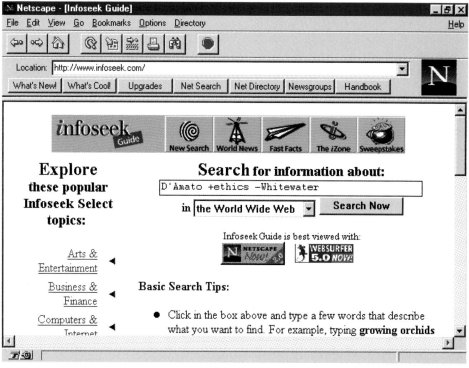

Figure 4.9 Infoseek is another good search service

Using the Inktomi Search Service

The Inktomi search service at **http://inktomi.berkeley.edu** works in a manner very similar to Infoseek or Yahoo. You can enter up to ten search terms, but common words and words shorter than four characters are ignored ("as," "is," "of," "and," "so," "on"). You need to precede search terms a web page must contain with the + character and precede terms a web page must not contain with the - character.

Using the Lycos Search Service

The Lycos search service at **http://www.lycos.com/** bills itself as the largest catalog to the Web. I'm not sure that's true. (For an interesting critique of the mathematics that Lycos uses to support its claim to fame, see the Inktomi search service web site referenced in the preceding paragraph.) But it is a very good site and works exactly

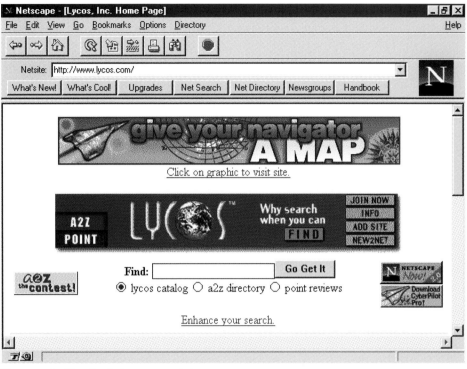

Figure 4.10 The simple Lycos search form

like you expect. Figure 4.10 shows the standard Lycos search form. You use its one text box to specify your search terms.

You can also use the simple Lycos search form's option buttons to specify what you want to search: the Lycos Catalog, the A2Z Directory, or the Point Reviews. The Lycos catalog indexes millions of web sites. The A2Z directory is a directory of web sites and pages organized by category. The Point Reviews option is a collection of roughly 50,000 web site reviews from which you can jump to the actual web sites reviewed.

If you want to provide instructions as to how Lycos should search its index, click the Enhance Your Search hyperlink so that Lycos displays the expanded search form shown in Figure 4.11.

The expanded Lycos search form, of course, requires search terms. But it also lets you specify how the Lycos search service uses these terms. Using the first Search Options drop-down list box, for

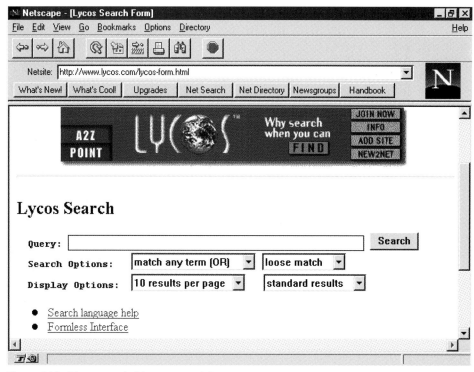

Figure 4.11 The expanded Lycos search form

example, you can specify whether Lycos should look for web pages that include all of your search terms, one of your search terms, or some specified number of search terms. You can also specify how selective, or picky, Lycos should be in its search by using the second Search Options drop-down list box.

Using the Magellan Search Service

The Magellan search service at **http://www.mckinley.com** works like the other search services. You enter your search term. If you want, you can provide additional instructions to the search service. And that's that. Or almost so. The Magellan search service does do one rather interesting thing. It attempts to identify web content of a, er, mature nature. So, while you can still find or stumble upon, for example, sexual web content using the Magellan search service, Magellan will identify which sites aren't mature and which are. You can also specify

**habits &
strategies**

To find an organization's web

page or web site, first try

guessing their URL, as

described in Chapter 3. If that

doesn't work, try one of the

commercial directories provided

by, for example, the Yahoo,

Lycos, or Alta Vista search

services.

that you want to restrict your search to web sites and web pages that aren't mature. (I guess that means you're looking for immature sites and pages?)

Using the Who Where Search Service

The Who Where search service at **http://www.whowhere.com** web site provides a directory of people and organizations. If you're trying to find some friend or associate's web page, you might want to try this first—although I've never had much luck actually finding people with this search service.

WHAT TO DO WHEN SEARCH SERVICES DON'T WORK

Despite their usefulness, search services aren't perfect. And they never will be. The content of the Internet is just too disorganized, diverse, and dynamic. For this reason, you should have some strategies for dealing with those situations in which you can't use a search service to find what you want. Let me give you some ideas:

- Recognize that you can't rely on search services. And for this reason, be sure you jot down the URL of an interesting web site you hear or read about.
- Try using both a directory and a search. I often find material one way that I couldn't find the other way.
- Try using a different search service. If you used Yahoo, for example, try Alta Vista, Inktomi, or Lycos.
- Take a wild guess as to a site's URL. (In the previous chapter, I provided some suggestions for guessing what an organization's web site URL is.)
- Read or at least review Chapters 7, 8, and 9 as well as the last three chapters (13, 14, and 15) of this book. Because it often is so hard to find what you're looking for, I've gone to quite a bit of effort to provide you with a multitude of interesting web sites. And they contain hyperlinks to point you to hundreds more!

ON FROM HERE

You should learn to use a search service really well. I kid you not. By taking the half hour or so required to gain proficiency, you'll save hours and hours. For this reason, I'd like to suggest that if you have more time, put this book down. Experiment with one or more of the search services. When you're done, we can spend a couple of quick chapters (Chapters 5 and 6) describing what happens when a hyperlink doesn't lead to another web page but instead leads to a Gopher server or an FTP server, or it starts a Telnet connection.

Electronic Mail, Mailing Lists, and Newsgroups

- Sending and receiving e-mail

- Subscribing to a mailing list

- Reading newsgroup articles

FAST FORWARD

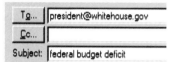

USING E-MAIL ➤ *pp. 63-65*

To send and receive e-mail messages, you need an e-mail client, and your Internet service provider needs to provide you with e-mail service.

COMPOSING AND READING
E-MAIL MESSAGES ➤ *p. 64*

Start your e-mail client. To compose your message, include the recipient's e-mail name, the subject of your message, and the text of your message. To read an e-mail message that someone else has sent you, double-click on it in the list of messages shown in your *inbox* or *in-basket*.

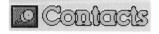

USING MAILING LISTS ➤ *pp. 66-68*

Mailing lists extend the Internet's e-mail feature. In essence, mailing lists are just newsletters or magazines that get published as a regular e-mail message. Mailing lists are usually free.

SUBSCRIBING TO MAILING LISTS ➤ *p. 67*

Find a mailing list you want to subscribe to (including the specific subscription instructions). Then send an e-mail message to the mailing list administrator or administrator program requesting you be added to the subscription list.

USING NEWSGROUPS ➤ *pp.68-71*

Newsgroups work much like mailing lists, except that rather than sending the same e-mail message to everyone on the mailing list, the message creator posts the message to an electronic bulletin board. To view a list of the newsgroups available on your Internet service provider's news server, you use your web browser.

The World Wide Web technically doesn't include Internet features such as e-mail, newsgroups, and mailing lists. However, you'll frequently encounter these other Internet features, because many hyperlinks lead to them. For this reason, you need to understand how these other features work and when you'll see them. (For more complete treatment of these topics, you might consider picking up a copy of *The Internet for Busy People* by Christian Crumlish (Osborne/McGraw-Hill, 1996).)

E-MAIL

E-mail, as you presumably know, lets you send little snippets of text to another computer user: the Queen of England, the President of the United States, your mother, me, or whomever. To send or create an e-mail message, you need an e-mail client—one called Microsoft Exchange comes with Windows 95, and another is built into Netscape version 2.0 and later—and your Internet service provider needs to provide you with e-mail service. (It almost certainly does.) Figure 5.1 shows what the Microsoft Exchange e-mail client looks like. If you take a quick gander at this figure, you'll notice that it really isn't anything special. You provide the recipient's e-mail name (you'll probably need to get this bit of information from the recipient). You describe the subject of your message. And you provide the text of your message. It's all quite simple.

Your e-mail client will also let you read e-mail messages that other people send you. In Microsoft Exchange, for example, you can see a list of the messages that other people have sent you by double-clicking the Inbox icon.

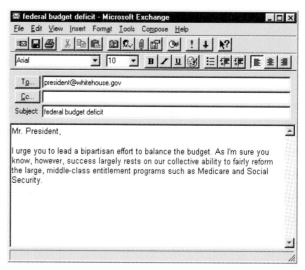

Figure 5.1 This is the Microsoft Exchange e-mail client, but other e-mail software looks and works the same way

Microsoft Exchange then displays the Inbox, a portion of which is shown here, which lists the e-mail messages you've received.

Netscape recommends you use Microsoft Exchange for e-mail if you're using Netscape version 1.x. If you're using Netscape version 2.x or later, your e-mail client is built into the Netscape browser. Internet Explorer, not surprisingly, uses Microsoft Exchange.

To read a message in your Inbox, double-click it. Figure 5.2 shows an actual e-mail message.

E-mail isn't actually part of the World Wide Web, but I wanted to provide this brief overview because some of the hyperlinks you click on a web page are *mailto links*. When you click a mailto link, your web browser software starts your e-mail client, and then fills in the e-mail address of the recipient, as shown in Figure 5.3.

At this point, all you have to do is provide an e-mail message subject description and type your message. You do this simply by clicking on the boxes into which you want to type text—and then you begin typing. Click the Send button when you finish.

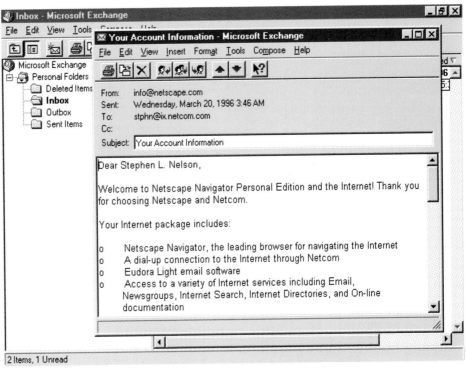

Figure 5.2 Microsoft Exchange displays each message in its own window

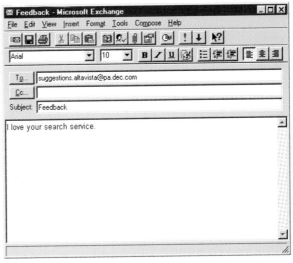

Figure 5.3 The Microsoft Exchange client, after clicking a mailto hyperlink

WHAT ARE MAILING LISTS?

My statement about mailing lists being like electronic newsletters or magazines is slightly inaccurate. In some cases, anyone who knows the e-mail name of the mailing list can send everyone on the mailing list a message.

Mailing lists extend the Internet's e-mail feature. In essence, mailing lists are just newsletters or magazines that get published as a regular e-mail message. For example, you might decide to create an electronic newsletter devoted to your favorite hobby. Perhaps it's nude skydiving. Once people learn about your mailing list, they might subscribe. And you would regularly—perhaps weekly or monthly—send an e-mail message to each subscriber.

Mailing lists are usually free (which makes sense because there's no real incremental cost to sending the e-mail messages to another subscriber). And you can get newsletters on just about any subject: vegetarianism, ferrets, Chevrolet Camaros, and so forth. For this reason—and even though they're not part of the World Wide Web—I suggest you take time to use the Publicly Accessible Mailing Lists web site, at **http://www.neosoft.com/internet/paml/bysubj.html** (see Figure 5.4).

Figure 5.4   The PAML web site organizes mailing lists by subject

CAUTION

Don't subscribe to more than one or two active mailing lists to start. If you do, you'll be deluged with e-mail messages.

To find a mailing list of interest, first page through the list of mailing list categories. Click on a category to get a list of mailing lists (see Figure 5.5).

To get more information about a particular mailing list—including the precise instructions for subscribing to the mailing list—click the mailing list name (see Figure 5.6). Usually, you simply send an e-mail message to a computer that automatically adds your e-mail name to the mailing list. Be very careful that you don't send your subscription request to the entire mailing list—it's sometimes possible to do this inadvertently if you don't pay attention to the subscription instructions.

Some mailing lists have a moderator, or gatekeeper, who filters the e-mail messages to the list. Other mailing lists let anyone send a message to the group. Generally, moderated lists are more interesting, because they stay more focused. And as a general rule, you should wait to send a message to a mailing list until you've had a chance to sense the tenor and tempo of the mailing list's current members. This practice of waiting and watching is called *lurking*.

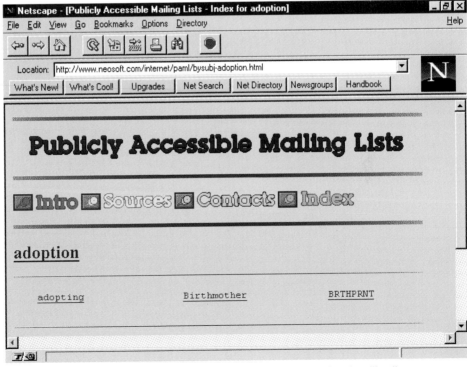

Figure 5.5   Click a subject, and the PAML web site displays the related mailing lists

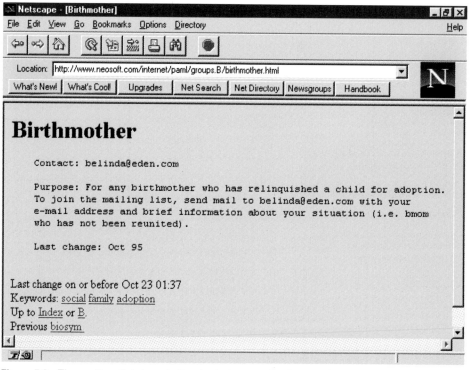

Figure 5.6 The mailing list description includes precise instructions for subscribing to a mailing list

WHAT ARE NEWSGROUPS?

Newsgroups work much like mailing lists, except that rather than sending the same e-mail message to everyone on the mailing list, the message creator posts the message to an electronic bulletin board (actually a special newsgroups news server). In this way, your inbox doesn't get cluttered with every message that every dingbat creates. You simply pick a bulletin board with messages that you're interested in—and then read only the messages you want. These bulletin boards, called *news-groups,* organize messages by subject.

Newsgroups aren't really part of the Web, but you'll want to understand what they are. Many of the search services also let you search newsgroup messages. Oftentimes,

CAUTION

Most of the really wild and truly bizarre content on the Internet is available through newsgroups. No matter what your political, religious, philosophical, or sexual values, you can find newsgroup content that offends you.

Because newsgroups aren't part of the World Wide Web—and don't use the http: protocol—their URLs look different, as shown in Figure 5.8.

the search services refer to the newsgroups as *Usenet*. What's more, some of the hyperlinks you click will also lead to newsgroups.

How you view newsgroups depends on your browser software. In Netscape version 1.*x*, you click the Newsgroups command button. In Netscape version 2.0 and later, you choose the Window|Netscape Mail command. In Internet Explorer, you click the Read Newsgroups toolbar button.

You may see a screen that asks which news server you want to use (if your Internet server provider supports more than one); if this is the case, you need to click one of the news servers. You'll see something that looks sort of like a web page (but actually isn't) that lists the newsgroups you've already subscribed to. (Probably your Internet service provider will have already subscribed to several popular newsgroups for you.) To see the articles listed in one of the news-groups to which you've already subscribed (such as the **news.newusers.questions** newsgroup), click it. Your web browser then displays a list of the e-mail messages that people have posted to the newsgroup (see Figure 5.7).

To see a posted message, click it. Figure 5.8 shows a message from the **news.newusers.questions** newsgroup.

Okay. Now you know what a newsgroup and a newsgroup message are. You should also know that newsgroups are a complete waste of time. Most of the messages aren't worth the time it takes to read them—let alone the time it takes to download them. And even when you do find some message with really interesting or useful information, you can't be sure that the information is good, true, accurate, or up to date. I rarely see good, useful information about small business management, computers, or personal finance—areas I hap-pen to have a professional interest in. And I can only assume that the same thing is true for many other newsgroup categories.

Newsgroups, however, are an extremely popular feature of the Internet, because they let people share information that they can't share in other ways. Through a trick called *Uuencode,* people can even post binary files (like graphic images or programs) to newsgroups. Uuencode converts a binary file to a text file so that it looks like a garbled message (see Figure 5.9). To convert a text file created by Uuencode back to its original binary format, you just reverse the process.

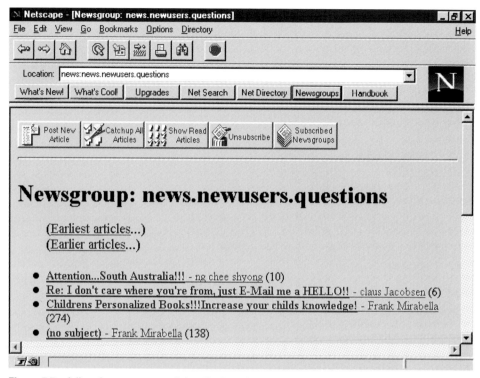

Figure 5.7   A list of newsgroup articles displayed with the Netscape 1.*x* browser

You can get a free copy of the Wincode program to Uuencode and Uudecode binary files from a web or FTP site that offers it. Search on the term **wincode** using a service like Alta Vista (see Chapter 4). Typically, these sites also provide wincode help.

Most of the sexual content available on the Internet is available through the newsgroups. And excepting the two or three newsgroups provided for new users, the **alt.sex.stories** and **alt.binaries.pictures.erotica** newsgroups are the most popular newsgroups. (Sorry Mom, but some readers are going to want to know this stuff.)

I'm not going to talk any more about newsgroups. But if you're interested, consider acquiring *The Internet for Busy People* book (men-

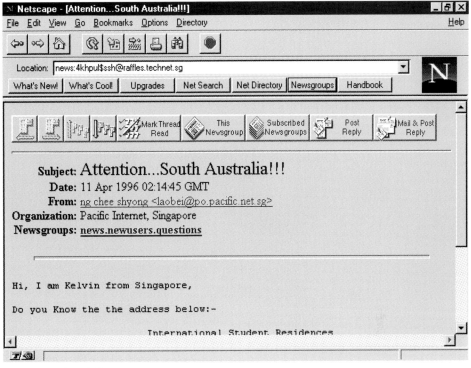

Figure 5.8 A real, live newsgroup message

tioned earlier in this chapter). It goes into a lot more detail about newsgroups.

ON FROM HERE

E-mail, mailing lists, and newsgroups aren't the only non-web Internet features you'll commonly find through hyperlinks. It's quite common to find yourself at an FTP site or Gopher server after clicking a hyperlink, for example. And, occasionally, you'll

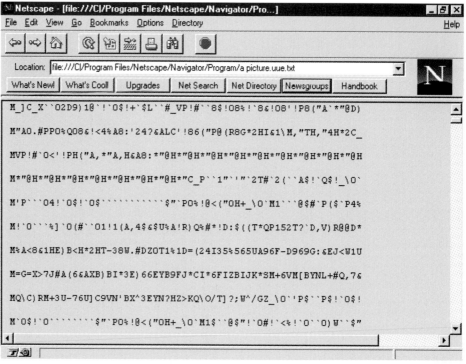

Figure 5.9 You can convert a binary file to a text-like code through a process called Uuencoding

also find yourself initiating a Telnet session by clicking a hyperlink. So the next chapter describes these other non-web Internet features.

FTP, Gopher, and Telnet

75

FAST FORWARD

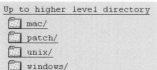

USING FTP ➤ *pp. 78-81*

FTP is another Internet service. It moves files between computers. Typically, you'll use FTP to move files from a free-to-the-public FTP server to your computer. If you want to find one of these free-to-the-public FTP servers, use a search service.

CONNECTING TO AN FTP SERVER ➤ *p. 78*

To connect to an FTP server, enter the FTP site's URL into the Location box. Or click a hyperlink that points to the FTP server.

DOWNLOADING FROM FTP ➤ *pp. 79-80*

To retrieve a file from an FTP site once you've connected, first find the file in the server's directories. Then double-click the file. Netscape will prompt you for the filename and location.

USING GOPHER ➤ *pp. 81-82*

Gopher organizes information resources—typically text files—using menus. To find a Gopher server, use a search service.

MAKING GOPHER CONNECTIONS ➤ *p. 81*

To connect to a Gopher server, enter the Gopher site's URL into the Location box. Or click a hyperlink that points to the Gopher server.

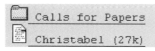

USING GOPHER RESOURCES ➤ *p. 82*

To view a Gopher resource at a Gopher site once you've connected:
1. Find the file in the server's directories.
2. Double-click the file.
3. If you want to save the file, choose the File|Save As command and, when Netscape prompts you, enter the filename and location.

Telnet - locis.loc.gov

Connect Edit Terminal Help

USING TELNET ➤ *pp. 82-86*

Telnet connects your computer to another computer system, in effect turning your computer into a terminal. To initiate a Telnet session, you click a Telnet hyperlink. To terminate a Telnet session, follow whatever instructions the Telnet host gives on ending your Telnet session. Then choose the Connect|Exit command.

As mentioned in the last chapter, some of the hyperlinks you click don't actually lead to other web pages or web sites. They cause you to move beyond the World Wide Web to other features, or services, of the Internet. This chapter really completes the discussion started in the last chapter by describing how you work with and use the other three Internet services you'll commonly encounter after clicking a hyperlink: FTP, Gopher, and Telnet.

This chapter briefly discusses FTP, Gopher, and Telnet. Again, if you want more information about these services and you like the Busy People book format, you might want to pick up a copy of Christian Crumlish's book, *The Internet for Busy People* (Osborne/McGraw-Hill, 1996), as I mentioned in Chapter 5.

WHAT IS FTP?

Let's start with FTP. *FTP,* which stands for *file transfer protocol,* moves files from one computer to another. While you might use FTP to move a file from your computer to some other computer—perhaps one halfway around the world—most people use FTP to grab files they need from free-to-the-public FTP servers operated by computer companies and universities. For example, you can often grab the newest beta, or test, copy of the Netscape Navigator program from FTP servers.

FTP servers aren't pretty to look at, as shown in Figure 6.1. In essence, they simply organize some distant computer's disk storage space into directories with files. Notice, by the way, that the URL shown in the Location box is different: it starts with the *ftp://* prefix to identify the site as an FTP server.

To move to a higher-level directory, you click the Up To Higher Level Directory hyperlink. To move to a lower-level directory—in other words, a subdirectory in the currently viewed directory—click a directory hyperlink.

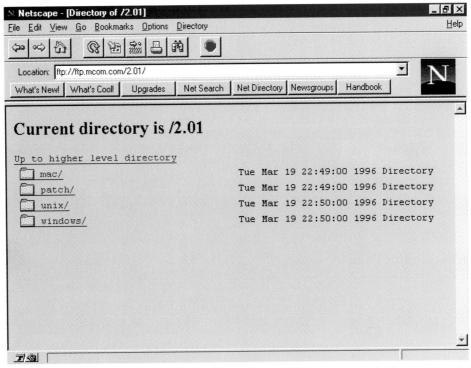

Figure 6.1 When you view an FTP server by using Netscape, the FTP server's directories and files appear in the program window

To retrieve one of the files listed at an FTP site, you click it. Netscape may not know what type of file it is, so it'll display a dialog box like the one shown here:

If Netscape recognizes the file—perhaps it's a graphic image file or something—it may just display the file in the Netscape program window.

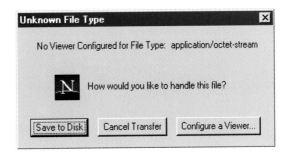

CAUTION

If you download files—and particularly if you download files from other than the most reputable FTP servers—you should probably acquire and regularly use an antivirus program. Refer to Chapter 10 for more information.

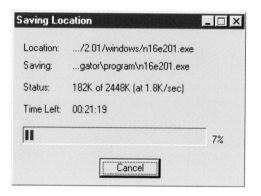

Simply click the Save To Disk button. When Netscape prompts you for a filename and location using the Save As dialog box, provide this information. Then click Save. Netscape, with the help of FTP, moves the file from the FTP server to your computer. As the FTP operation progresses, Netscape reports on the progress using the dialog box shown here:

The FTP service sounds great, of course, until you realize that the chance that you'll know both the precise name and location of some file is infinitesimally small. And I'm with you on this. I rarely use FTP to do anything really productive or worthwhile. Nevertheless, FTP can still be useful. Software companies like Microsoft and Netscape Communications routinely put new versions of programs that make up their operating systems and application programs on their FTP servers. And sometimes a call to a software company's technical support people will elicit the response, "Well, you just need to download the *thing*.zip file from our FTP server." But once you know the URL of the FTP site and the name of the file, it's easy to download a file. You just click the filename or description. Sometimes you can also download a file directly from a web page just by clicking a hyperlink.

By the way, most of the files you download with FTP are compressed using a program called PKZIP or one of its cousins, such as WINZIP. A compression program scrunches a file so it's smaller, takes less disk space, and transmits more quickly over a network connection. (You can also scrunch several files together so they all fit inside of one, smaller compressed file.) You'll always be able to tell if this is so,

There are other file-compression utilities, but you don't see them all that frequently in the IBM-compatible environment.

habits & strategies

You find FTP and Gopher sites in the same way that you find web sites and web pages—with a URL, a hyperlink, or a search service.

because the file will use the *.zip* file extension. So if you download a *zipped* file—this is what people call them—you'll need to unzip the file before you can use it. You can order a copy of PKZIP from PKWARE, Inc. at (414) 355-8699. You can order a copy of WINZIP from PsL (even though WINZIP is made by Nico Mak Computing) at (713) 524-6394.

WHAT IS GOPHER?

Gopher servers—such as Carnegie-Mellon University's server at **gopher://english-server.hss.cmu.edu** shown in Figure 6.2—organize information using menus. Typically, Gopher menus organize topics by category. If you select a particular category, Gopher displays another menu of subtopics within the selected category and information files. For example, Figure 6.3 shows the menu that appears if you choose the 18th-Century item from the menu shown in Figure 6.2. Notice that the URL shown in the Location box starts with the *gopher://* prefix to identify the site as a Gopher server.

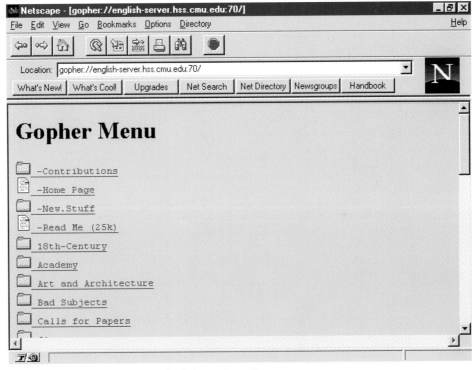

Figure 6.2 Gopher menus organize information using menus

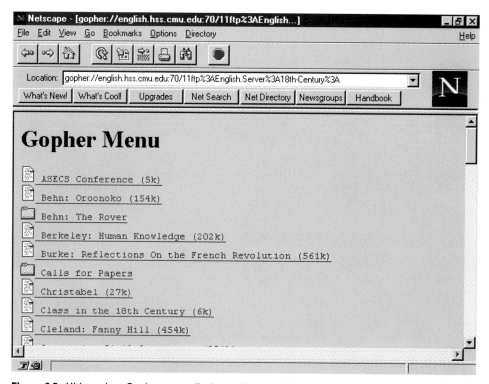

Figure 6.3 Ultimately, a Gopher menu displays a listing of information resources—usually text files

If you look closely at Figure 6.3 above, you'll notice that some of the items listed use a folder-like icon. If you select these items, Gopher displays still another menu. You'll also notice that other items use a page-like icon. If you select one of these items, Gopher opens a text file. If you select the seventh item, "Christabel," in Figure 6.3, Gopher opens a text file that holds Coleridge's poem (see Figure 6.4).

If you want to save the text file a Gopher menu item displays, choose the File|Save As command. Then, when Netscape prompts you for a filename and location, provide this information.

WHAT IS TELNET?

Telnet is, well, weird. If you click a Telnet hyperlink, Netscape starts a Telnet session—which means that your computer, in effect, works as if it's just a terminal connected to some other big computer. Telnet isn't very popular—and it's sort of pooh-poohed because it's

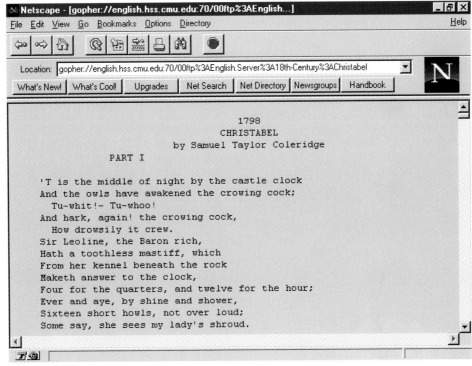

Figure 6.4 Coleridge wrote *Christabel* with quill and ink, and two centuries later still makes us think

not graphical and it's old (as far as Internet protocols, or services, go). But I actually think Telnet is pretty useful. It often leads to computer systems—such as the United States Library of Congress—that have great information resources stored on rather outdated systems.

To use Telnet with Netscape, you first need to set it up as a Helper application. To do this in Netscape version 1.*x*, choose the Options|Preferences command, and click the Applications And Directories tab (see Figure 6.5). Or, in Netscape version 2.0 or later, choose the Options|General Preferences command and click the Apps tab. Next, enter the complete path name for the Telnet program into the Telnet Application text box. If you're using the Telnet program that comes with Windows 95 and if you installed Windows 95 into the Windows directory, or folder, you should enter **c:\windows\ telnet.exe** into the Telnet Application text box.

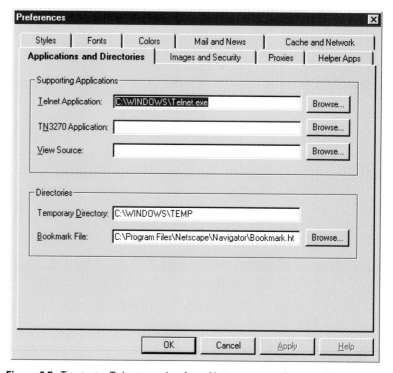

Figure 6.5 To start a Telnet session from Netscape, you first need to tell Netscape which Telnet application you want to use

habits & strategies

As you log on to a Telnet server, you may be asked for your user name and a password. Convention is to supply your user name as "anonymous" and your password as your complete e-mail name.

When you click a Telnet hyperlink, Netscape opens the Telnet helper application (see Figure 6.6), which is just another program that acts as the Telnet client.

Once you start Telnet, you issue commands to the Telnet server in whatever form it expects—but often by selecting commands from numbered menus. This is how you issue commands to the LOCIS Telnet site shown in Figure 6.6, for example. (I can't give you precise instructions for working with various Telnet servers, because they're all different.)

When you want to terminate your Telnet session, first follow any instructions from the Telnet server on terminating the Telnet session. Then choose the Connect|Disconnect command. If you want to stop the Telnet program, choose the Connect|Exit command.

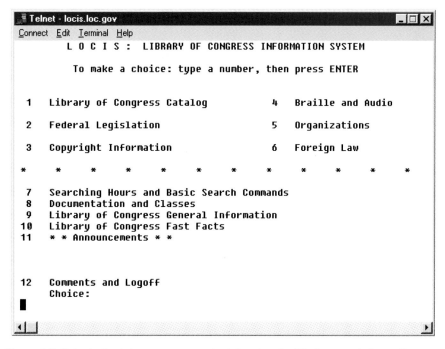

Figure 6.6 Telnet clients turn your computer into a terminal that connects to another computer system

If you can't get the Telnet program to work right, choose the Terminal|Preferences command. Then use the Terminal Preferences dialog box, shown here, to tell the Telnet client how the Telnet server wants to work with your computer.

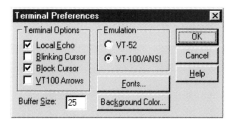

You need to make sure, for example, that whatever emulation the Telnet server wants—VT-52 or VT-100/ANSI—is what the Telnet program uses. (Try VT-100/ANSI emulation first, if you have questions.) You may also need to fiddle with the Terminal Options settings. For example, if you don't see anything in the window, mark the Local Echo check box. And if you see every letter twice, as in

Pprreess HH ttoo ggeett hheellpp!!

unmark the Local Echo check box. You may also need to fiddle with one of the other options in a way I can't guess, so click the Terminal Preferences dialog box's Help button if you have further questions.

ON FROM HERE

This chapter completes our discussion of the World Wide Web's mechanics. You actually know everything you need to successfully and expeditiously explore the web. However, I can still save you quite a bit of time by giving you some very specific ideas and instructions for using the web in certain ways. And that's what I do in the three chapters that follow.

CHAPTER 7

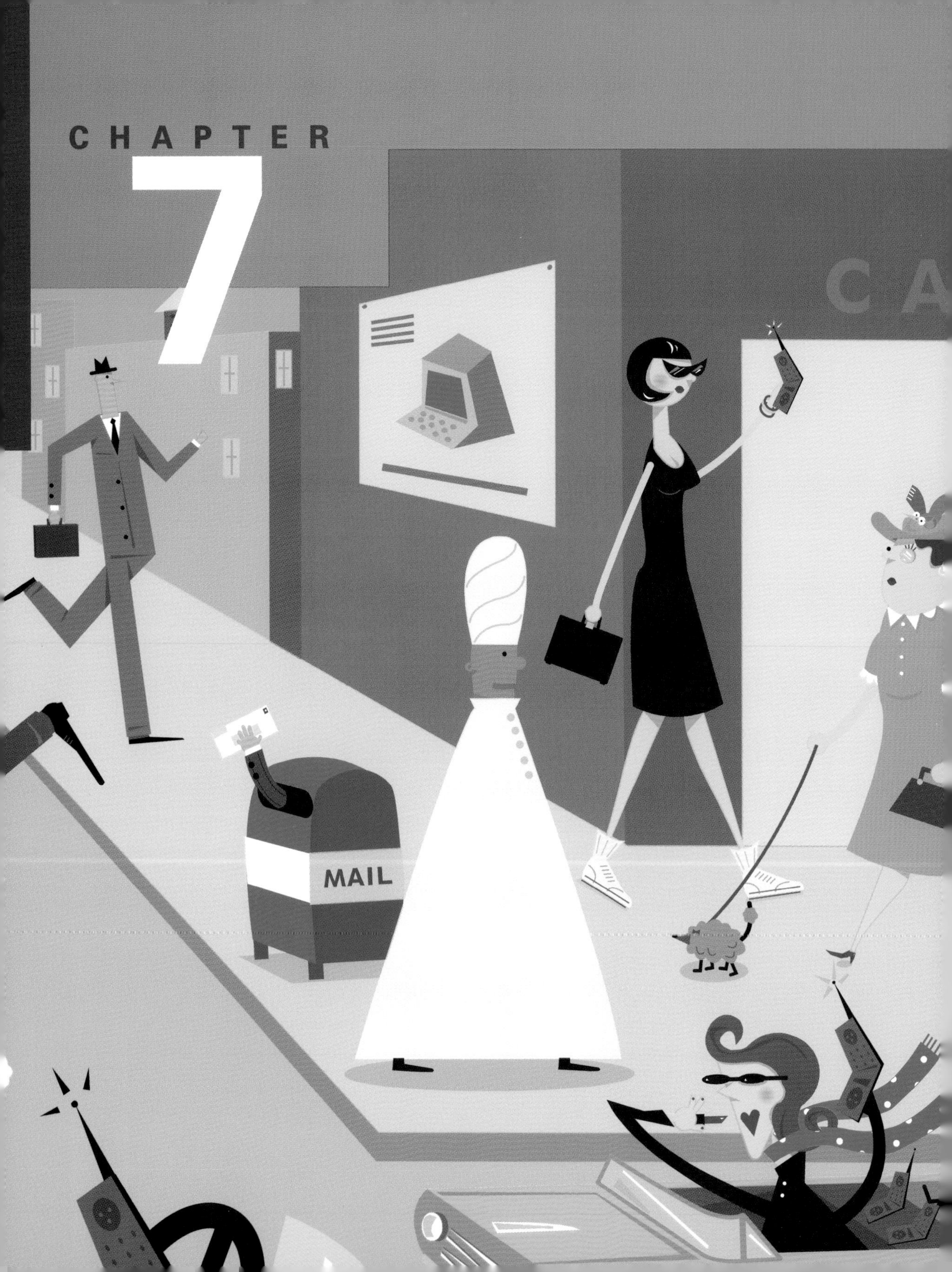

Money Management with the Web

INCLUDES

- Finding a new or better job

- Planning your retirement

- Buying or financing a home

- Insuring against financial disasters

- Buying and financing a car

- Planning kids' college expenses

FAST FORWARD

FINDING A NEW OR BETTER JOB ➤ *pp. 92-95*

You may be able to find a job using the America's Job Bank web site. To view the America's Job Bank web site, enter **http://www.ajb.dni.us** as the URL.

PLANNING YOUR RETIREMENT ➤ *pp. 95-96*

There isn't as much retirement planning information available on the Web as you might think. The Vanguard Group web site at **http://www.vanguard.com/**, however, provides volumes of useful investment and financial planning information.

Funds

BUYING AND FINANCING A HOME ➤ *pp. 96-97*

Unfortunately, there's no web site you can go to that lists all of the homes for sale in your community or the current interest rates offered by all of your local real estate lenders. However, the Financenter web site at **http://www.financenter.com/** provides a bunch of financial calculators that you can use to determine how much mortgage you can afford and what your monthly mortgage payment will be.

BUYING LIFE INSURANCE ➤ *pp. 98-99*

You can calculate precisely how much life insurance you need by using a form at the Accuquote web site. To get there, enter the URL **http://www.accuquote.com/** into the Location box; then click the Life Insurance Needs Calculator.

BUYING AND FINANCING A CAR ➤ *pp. 101-103*

There are numerous web sites that provide information for car shoppers. To view the DealerNet web pages, for example, enter **http://www.dealernet.com/** as the URL. To view the IntelliChoice web site, enter **http://www.intellichoice.com/** as the URL.

Education

PLANNING FOR YOUR KIDS' COLLEGE EXPENSES ➤ *pp. 103-105*

You can get information about college costs, admissions procedures, financial aid—and just about anything else—from the CollegeAssist web site. To view the CollegeAssist web site, enter **http://www.edworks.com/** as the URL.

INVESTMENT ANALYSIS AND DECISION-MAKING ➤ *pp. 105-109*

If you're looking for basic investment information, visit the web site at **http://nearnet.gnn.com/gnn/meta/finance/feat/21st/ index.html**. If you're an active investor who buys individual stocks and bonds, visit CNN's financial news network web site: **http://cnnfn.com/**.If you want financial information about a specific U.S. publicly held company, you should visit the Securities and Exchange Commission's EDGAR web site: **http://www.sec.gov/edgarhp.htm**.

The Web provides a bunch of pages that promise to improve your personal finances. You can use the Web to find a new job or a better job, for example. You can get information that lets you make better decisions about retirement, buying a home, or choosing a mortgage. And you can even become more sophisticated in your investing—using the Web as another source of investment and insurance information.

You and I will talk about all of this in the chapter that follows, but I want to warn you before we begin that you need to take everything you read on the Web with a grain a salt. Because you're rarely paying for the financial information you get from the Web, most everything you see will be an advertisement for a product or service. And that's okay, I guess. But it also means the way web publishers are really making money is by getting you to buy their product or service—and that may not be the smart money thing to do. I'll talk about this web weirdness more in the pages that follow.

habits & strategies

Even if you aren't looking for a new job, the America's Job Bank web site could be helpful. For example, if you were negotiating a new salary with your current employer, you could see what other employers are paying for similar jobs.

FINDING A NEW OR BETTER JOB

You may be able to find a job by using the Web. No joking. The U.S. Department of Labor, in collaboration with state employment agencies, set up something called America's Job Bank. It lists roughly a quarter of a million jobs available throughout the country. To view the America's Job Bank web page (see Figure 7.1), enter **http://www.ajb.dni.us** as the URL.

Once the America's Job Bank web page appears, click on the Menu Search hyperlink. This tells the America's Job Bank web server that you want to begin searching through its job listings. Next you'll use list boxes to identify the type of job you're looking for and the states in which you'd be willing to work. Using this information, America's Job

Figure 7.1 The America's Job Bank web pages describe roughly 250,000 jobs available throughout the United States

Bank prepares a list of job titles and salaries (see Figure 7.2). To get more information about one of these listed jobs, you mark the job's check box and then click the View Jobs button.

Let me mention a handful of other useful job-search web sites, too. The web site **http://www.careerpath.com/** provides newspaper employment ads from the *Boston Globe, Chicago Tribune, Los Angeles Times, New York Times, San Jose Mercury,* and *Washington Post.* (Last I checked, in fact, this web site had over 40,000 job advertisements.)

The web site at **http://www.espan.com/** works slightly differently. It first interviews you to gauge your credentials and qualifications. Once it has this information, it searches its database of job openings for appropriate positions.

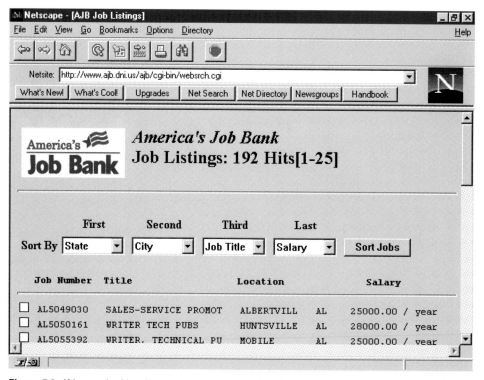

Figure 7.2 If I were looking for a technical writer job, this list would both identify jobs and give me an idea about starting salaries

The web site at **http://www.occ.com/** provides one other source of job listings information. Billed as the Internet's most frequently accessed career center, the Online Career Center is a nonprofit association of a bunch of large and technology-savvy corporations. It lets you explore job listings by industry and location. You can also post an online resume (which might just get reviewed by some corporate recruiter looking for someone like you).

Finally, I want to give you one other job hunting idea. While a job-based search for employment may seem like the way to go, you may also want to use an employer-based search. In other words, rather than saying you want a job as, say, a technical writer, you could say that you want a job with a particular employer such as Microsoft or IBM. In this case, you should visit the employer's web site, as it may provide job information. You may be able to guess the URL for a particular employer. For example, **http://www.microsoft.com/** is Microsoft's URL. And **http://www.ibm.com/** is IBM's URL. If you can't guess the web site's URL, use one of the search services such as Yahoo (described in Chapter 4) to search for the employer's web site.

PLANNING YOUR RETIREMENT

There isn't as much retirement planning information available on the Web as you might think. Oh, sure. If you use one of the search indexes like, say, Yahoo, to search on the words "retirement planning," you'll get thousands of hits. But much of what you'll find, should you start exploring this stuff, are advertisements for people who want to sell you retirement planning services or products (like annuities, personal financial plans, and mutual funds). These web pages probably help the advertisers prepare for their retirements—but I'm not sure they help you prepare for yours.

One major exception to the previous generalization, however, is the Vanguard Group web site at **http://www.vanguard.com/**. Vanguard operates a wonderful web site that provides volumes of useful investment and financial planning information. I heartily recommend you visit this site for retirement planning information.

Retirement planning, it turns out, requires that you ask and answer two deceptively simple questions. You need to decide how much you should save to fund your retirement. And, you need to decide where you should invest this money.

To answer the first question, you must make some rather complicated financial calculations taking into account the years over which you'll save, the annual return your savings will produce, and how long you'll be retired. Fortunately, Vanguard's web site includes a retirement calculator which helps you make these calculations. To view the Vanguard retirement planner, enter **http://www.vanguard.com/tools/ retire.html** as the URL. The Vanguard retirement planner lets you take an investment risk test, which gauges your sensitivity to the vagaries of the financial markets, and then lets you map out a retirement savings program based on the type of investments you're willing to use for your retirement savings (see Figure 7.3).

The Vanguard Group, as you may know, is a no-load mutual fund management company. Their corporate mission is to provide low-cost investment management services to investors.

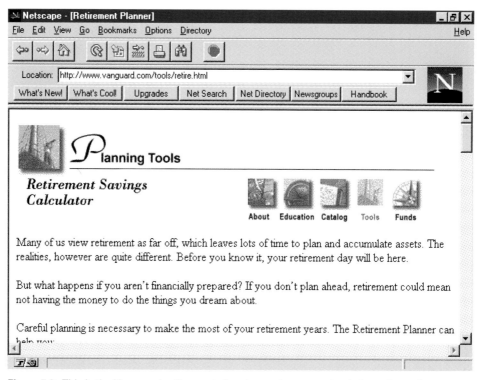

Figure 7.3 This is the Vanguard retirement planning web page; to begin inputting retirement planning data, scroll down the page

The second part to retirement planning is deciding how you should invest your money. Vanguard's investor education web pages also provide wonderful information on retirement planning. For example, the web page at **http://www.vanguard.com/educ/lib/bogle/retire.html** provides a useful primer on retirement investing. What's more, you can (and should!) poke around a bit to see what new retirement planning information Vanguard has placed at their web site.

BUYING AND FINANCING A HOME

The Internet can't help you with many of the biggest decisions you'll want to make as you buy a home. For example, there's no web site you can go to that lists all of the homes for sale in your community. And even if such a list were available, transmission times are still too slow to make it worthwhile to sit in front of your computer endlessly downloading huge graphical images. You're much better off watching a home-for-sale cable television show (available in many areas) or, surprise, actually visiting open houses.

As concerns the other big decision you'll make—choosing a mortgage—it also turns out the Web isn't all that useful. Because small differences in interest rates make huge differences in your interest expenses over the life of a loan (for example, with a $100,000 mortgage, an eighth of a percent difference in interest rates produces a $10,000 difference in interest costs over the life of a loan), be sure that you check mortgage interest rates available from all of your local real estate lenders. Currently there is no national database of local real estate lenders. So, unfortunately, you can't search some database of mortgage interest rates and find the lender with the lowest annual percentage rate. In fact, I wouldn't even waste time searching online for low mortgage interest rates. What I'd suggest is to find a reputable local mortgage broker and have them find the cheapest mortgage for you.

So, does all of the foregoing mean that there's no online help for home buyers and mortgage borrowers? Well, not quite. At least one web site provides financial calculators that you can use to determine how much mortgage you can afford and what your monthly mortgage payment will be. To visit this web site, enter **http://www.financenter.com/** into the Location box (see Figure 7.4). To see a list of home financing calculators, click the A Home hyperlink.

habits & strategies

The annual percentage rate (APR) shows total loan costs—interest, loan fees, discount points, and so on—as a percentage of the loan amount. If you repay a loan in the regular term, the loan with the lowest APR is the cheapest.

INSURING AGAINST FINANCIAL DISASTERS

For most people, there are five general categories of insurance needed: life insurance, disability insurance, property insurance (including car, homeowners, renters, marine, and so forth), health insurance, and personal liability insurance. These types differ, so I'll discuss them separately in the paragraphs that follow.

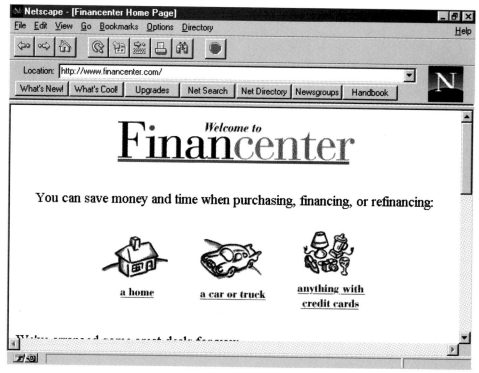

Figure 7.4 The Financenter web site provides handy financial calculators that you can use to assist you in your home purchase and financing decisions

Life Insurance

This is morbid, I know. I don't like thinking about my mortality, either. But here's the reality. If other people depend on your income—like your spouse or kids or life partner or whoever—you generally need life insurance so that the insurance proceeds (along with earnings on those proceeds) can replace the income you would have earned.

People use all sorts of crazy rules of thumb to estimate how much life insurance you need. But that's stupid, because you can calculate precisely how much life insurance you need by using a computer. In fact, the Accuquote web site lets you do just this. To get there, enter the URL **http://www.accuquote.com/** into the Location box. Then click the Life Insurance Needs Calculator hyperlink to get to a form that collects the information you needed to make the life insurance calculation. Figure 7.5 shows a portion of the form you'll work with.

Once you determine how much life insurance you need, you should shop around for the cheapest renewable term life insurance available from an insurer rated A or better by A.M. Best. (A.M. Best rates the financial soundness of insurance companies.) You can also get a free quote by e-mailing a request to the Accuquote folks. (For fun, I really tried this and got a really good price on some cheap term life insurance.)

Disability Insurance

You probably also need disability insurance—perhaps more than you need life insurance. Unfortunately, I've never been able to find really

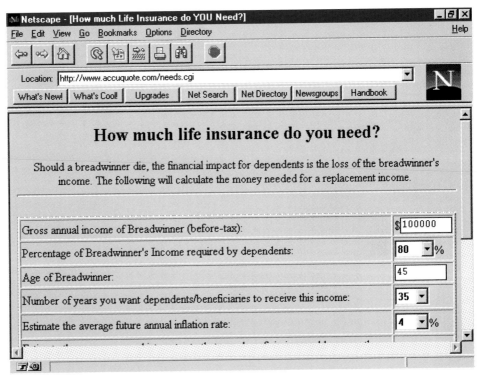

Figure 7.5 The Accuquote web site supplies a form you can use to calculate precisely how much life insurance you need

good information about disability insurance on the Internet. There is an insurance company that specializes in disability insurance, and they've got a pretty good web site at **http://www.paulrevere.com/** that describes why you need disability insurance. But most of what's out there are advertisements for insurance agents who want to sell you disability insurance (as well as other products). This isn't bad, but there's no real benefit to finding your agent via the Web rather than in some other way—such as from a friend's referral.

Let me make just two more quick observations about disability insurance. Short-term disability coverage is prohibitively expensive. Therefore, if you can find a way to accumulate a substantial rainy-day fund (one equal to three to six month's living expenses), you can skip the short-term disability insurance and instead look at just long-term disability insurance (which is far cheaper).

Don't just talk to insurance agents. If you belong to a professional society, fraternal organization, or union, it's very possible that you can get good, cheap, long-term disability insurance there. For example, I get really cheap long-term disability insurance from the American Institute of Certified Public Accountants, a professional society I belong to. For not much more than $100 a year, I get a policy that would, after the three-month waiting period, pay me $5,000 a month (tax-free) for the rest of my life.

Property, Health, and Personal Liability Insurance

I've searched around and haven't been able to find any good, general information on property insurance either. That's not to say that you don't need this insurance. You very well may. There just isn't any good general information available—at least none that I could find. And there aren't really any computer-based tools for making these decisions. You'll need to research these insurance categories the old-fashioned way: by talking with insurance agents and ultimately finding someone you can trust.

By the way, there is a web site called the Insurance Shopping Network at **http://www.800insureme.com/** that lets you get online quotes on auto, home, health, and life insurance. You fill out an onscreen form, send the Insurance Shopping Network this information, and then get a quote in the form of an e-mail message. You may be able to save some money by getting quotes from several insurers, so you may want to look into this service.

An Insurance Planning Caveat

Let me close our little discussion about insurance with a caveat. One of the ways you save money when it comes to insurance is by minimizing the insurance you purchase and bearing as much risk as you can. For example, it often makes sense to purchase a major medical health insurance policy rather than a full coverage policy. It often makes sense to drop life and disability coverage as you get older if your retirement and other savings are substantial. And there are all sorts of extra whistles and bells offered by agents and insurers that you often shouldn't buy: cancer insurance, medical or uninsured motorist riders that are part of a car policy, and investment or cash value accounts that are part of life insurance policies.

Nobody makes any money by telling you not to buy something, however. As a result, there's little incentive for insurance companies to provide you with web sites that explain how to buy less insurance. And the same thing is true for insurance agents selling coverage. Yet often your best course of action is to judiciously reduce insurance coverage by choosing to bear certain acceptable financial risks yourself.

BUYING AND FINANCING A CAR

Because I'm planning on buying a new car shortly, one of my favorite web sites is DealerNet web site (see Figure 7.6). My wife doesn't like the time I spend ogling shiny new sedans, coupes, and sport-utility vehicles. But, man, I have some fun. To view the DealerNet web pages, enter the **http://www.dealernet.com/** as the URL. When the page appears, click either the New Cars or Used Cars button to start your search.

Note, too, that the DealerNet home page also provides a link to car financing sources. You can use the information you get by following this link to explore alternative financing sources. And even if you choose to use some other financing source—your local bank, say, or the credit union at work—you'll still benefit from knowing what other lenders are charging.

CAUTION

Since all its hyperlinks are clickable images, the DealerNet web site doesn't really work for text-only viewing. This is unfortunate—the site is s-l-o-w. Chapter 10 describes how to use text-only viewing to improve transmission times.

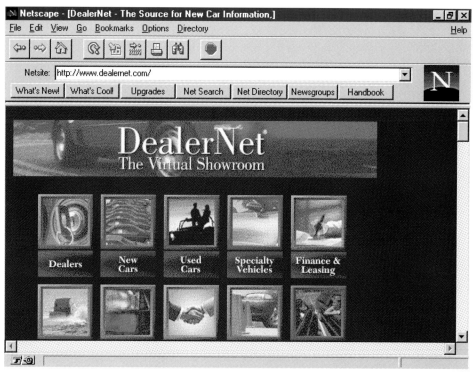

Figure 7.6 The DealerNet web page lets you describe what you're looking for by using a form and then, once you submit your query, presents you with a list of cars meeting your criteria

The Financenter web site mentioned earlier also offers financial calculators you can use to compare the costs of leasing a car and buying a car.

If you want more detailed information about a particular vehicle—say it's the one you've pretty much chosen—you may want to visit the IntelliChoice web site. While the DealerNet site provides lots of interesting information about most vehicles, that information comes from the manufacturer or car dealer. By comparison, the IntelliChoice web site provides data about all sorts of things the manufacturer or car dealer may not want you to know: the costs of operating the vehicle, the manufacturer's invoice price to the dealer, the number of problems existing owners are having, the risk that someone will steal the car, the chance an accident results in a fatality, and so on.

To view the IntelliChoice web site (see Figure 7.7), enter the URL **http://www.intellichoice.com/** into the Location box. You'll be given a choice of either a free partial report or a full report on some vehicle.

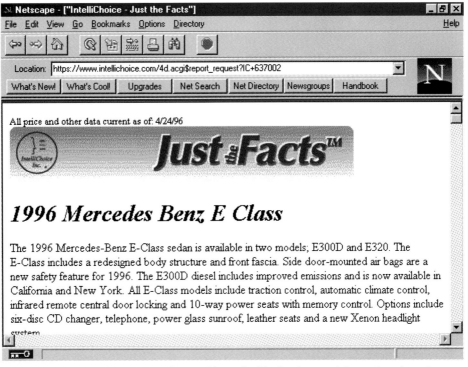

Figure 7.7 The IntelliChoice web site provides valuable, hard-to-get information about the car or cars you may purchase

A full report costs $4.95 at this writing, which you pay by supplying your credit card number.

PLANNING FOR YOUR KIDS' COLLEGE EXPENSES

You can get information about college costs, admissions procedures, financial aid—and just about anything else—from the CollegeAssist web site, shown in Figure 7.8. Enter the URL **http://www.edworks.com/** into the Location text box to visit there.

You'll need to do a bit of exploring here to find what you're looking for, but CollegeAssist is pretty handy. They provide an online database of colleges that you can search based on location, cost, educational

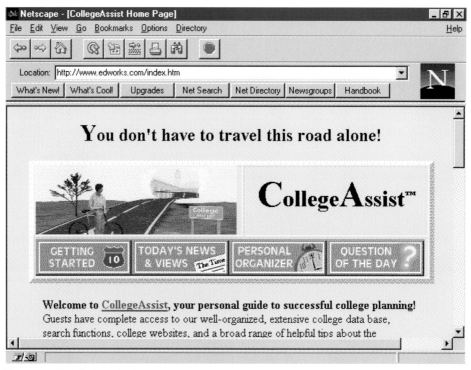

Figure 7.8 The CollegeAssist web site lets you describe the sort of college you're looking for and then build a list of colleges matching your search criteria

You can pay an extra $40 or so annually to gain additional college planning services from the CollegeAssist web site.

emphasis, and so forth. (CollegeAssist charges colleges around $300 a year to appear on their list—which is pretty cheap—so you'll probably find information about whatever college you're interested in there.)

If you're trying to figure out how much you should begin saving for your two-year-old prodigy's college fund—you can use a slick little trick for making your calculations. Consider college as a four-year period of retirement for your young scholar, with required retirement income equal to the annual college costs you'll want to pay from your savings. Once you make this paradigm shift, you can use the Vanguard web site's retirement planning calculator to figure out what you need to save. (I described that web site and provided its URL in the "Planning Your Retirement" section.)

If it's too late to begin saving—say young Imelda begins college in a few months—you can get information about the financial aid process online, but I'm not sure that's such a good idea. What you'll

CAUTION

CollegeAssist offers data on more than 1,600 four-year public and private colleges, but not on two-year community colleges. That's unfortunate—community colleges can be a wonderful way to start a college education and save money.

The online book, Frank Armstrong's Investment Strategies for the 21st Century, *includes chapters on investing for retirement and college costs.*

really run into are financial aid consultants who charge you money for helping you fill out the forms and helping you structure your family finances in way that potentially maximizes your eligibility. I personally have a problem with people managing the system this way. But more importantly, if you choose to do this, I think it makes more sense to get a referral from a friend who's actually worked with one of these consultants.

While we're on the subject, I may as well also tell you that unless you're raising a family on a modest income—say less than $20,000 a year—there's not any free money for college. When people refer to financial aid, what they almost always mean are loans. There is no free lunch.

Before I wrap up this discussion of college planning, however, let me point out that most universities and colleges maintain their own web sites. If you're considering a particular school (or your young scholar is), be sure to visit the institution's web site to get more information.

The place to start your search is at Yahoo's Universities list (see Figure 7.9) at the **http://www.yahoo.com/Education/Universities** URL. Once there, click on the United States in the list of countries, then enter the name of the university you want to research in the text box, mark the Search Only In Universities option button, and click Search.

INVESTMENT ANALYSIS AND DECISION-MAKING

If you are looking for basic investment information, there is a pretty good series of articles written by Frank Armstrong and published online on the Internet by GNN. To read these articles, enter **http://nearnet.gnn.com/gnn/meta/finance/feat/21st/index.html** into the Location box. This URL leads you to an index of articles about modern investing (see Figure 7.10). I don't agree with everything Armstrong says, but his material is the best I've seen online.

Another good source of general investment information is the Investment FAQ, which collects interesting and valuable posts from the misc.investment newsgroup. You never know what sort of content you'll get in a newsgroup. Often, the content is very poor. This collection of investment-related articles, however, is really quite good. To view it,

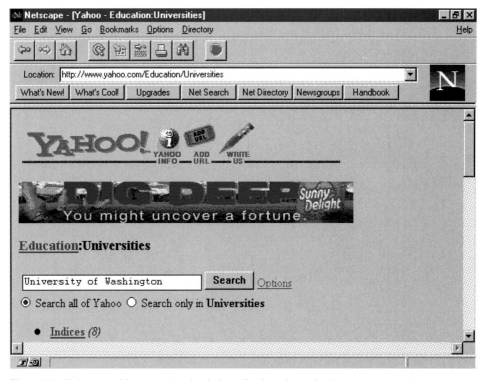

Figure 7.9 Yahoo provides an extensive index of university web sites you can use to research colleges and universities you or a child may attend

enter the URL **http://www.centcon.com/~billman/faqindex.html** into the Location box.

If you're interested specifically in mutual fund investing, you should visit the Online version of *Mutual Funds Magazine* (see Figure 7.11). To do this, enter **http://www.mfmag.com/** into the Location box. You'll need to subscribe to get full access to the site's information, but at least at this writing, subscription was free.

If you're an active investor who buys individual stocks and bonds, you'll be thrilled with the investment information available on the Web. In fact, there's so much information available that I'm not sure where I should start. Perhaps the best way to begin is by providing the URL for CNN's financial news network web site: **http://cnnfn.com/**. (Don't include that last period, of course.) I think the CNNFN web site may just be the best financial news web site there is.

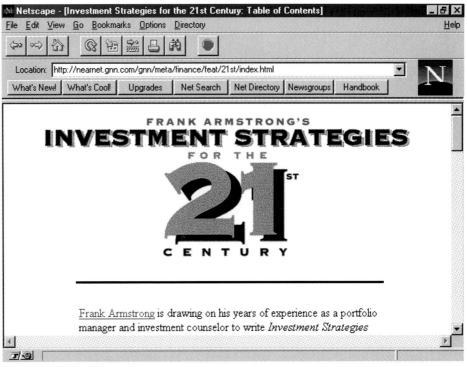

Figure 7.10 Frank Armstrong's web page offers a index of solid articles about investing

**habits &
strategies**

Don't research individual stocks

until you understand the

info in the Frank Armstrong's

online book. Otherwise, read

Burton Malkiel's, A Random

Walk Down Wall Street.

The *Wall Street Journal* provides a pretty good web site at **http://update.wsj.com/**, but you need to subscribe before you can use the site. You don't pay anything to subscribe—or at least you don't do this yet. You do, however, provide a bit of personal information about yourself. One very useful feature of the *Wall Street Journal*'s web site is that news stories contain hyperlinks to what are called "briefing books." A briefing book describes a company in detail. For example, if you're reading an article and come across a reference to AT&T, you'll see that this company name is actually a hyperlink. When you click the hyperlink, you get additional information about AT&T. (At this writing, briefing books were free, but that will probably have changed by the time you read this.)

If you want financial information about a specific, U.S. publicly held company, you should visit the Securities and Exchange Commission's EDGAR web site. For individual investors, it provides online

Figure 7.11 The Online edition of *Mutual Funds Magazine* provides detailed data on over 7,000 mutual funds and contains hyperlinks to many mutual fund management companies' web sites

access to the quarterly and annual reports that all U.S. publicly held companies must file with the Securities and Exchange Commission. (The EDGAR system also allows publicly held companies to submit their financial data, too.) To visit EDGAR, enter the URL **http://www.sec.gov/edgarhp.htm** into the Location box. Figure 7.12 shows an example of the sort of information you can view using the EDGAR system.

Before I close this discussion of investment analysis and decision-making, let me also emphasize what may be obvious. If you're interested in investing in a particular company, you should visit their web site (if they have one). You typically won't find financial information there, but you do get access to lots of information about the firm's products and services. You can usually easily locate a particular firm's web site by using one of the search indexes—such as Yahoo—and entering the company name as your search keyword.

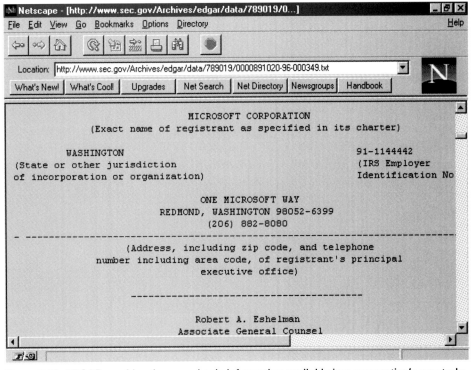

Figure 7.12 EDGAR provides the same basic information available in a corporation's quarterly and annual filings with the SEC

ON FROM HERE

I have mixed feelings about using the Web for money management. While it's true that there are wonderful resources available, it's also true that you have to wade through an awful lot of guck to get to the good stuff. I've tried to point you in the right direction in this chapter—and steer you away from the garbage—but you still need to be careful. Enough said.

Healthier Living with the Web

INCLUDES

- Quitting smoking

- Help with alcohol problems

- Losing weight

- Eating healthier foods

- Fitness and exercise

- Having a baby

- Help with special medical problems and conditions

FAST FORWARD

QUITTING SMOKING ➤ *pp. 114-115*

Get information and help about quitting smoking from the Ashtray web site at **http://web.bu.edu:80/COHIS/smoking/smoke.htm**.

ADDRESSING ALCOHOL PROBLEMS ➤ *p. 116*

Visit the Alcoholics Anonymous web site at **http://www.alcoholics-anonymous.org/** or the Al-Anon/Alateen web site at **http://solar.rtd.utk.edu/~al-anon/** for help in dealing with alcohol problems—yours or someone else's.

GETTING NUTRITION AND WEIGHT LOSS INFORMATION ➤ *pp. 116-117*

Start with the U.S. Food and Drug Administration's Center for Food Safety and Applied Nutrition web site at **http://vm.cfsan.fda.gov/list.html** if you want nutrition information or advice on common dieting and weight loss strategies.

GETTING AND STAYING PHYSICALLY FIT ➤ *pp. 117-118*

Look for general fitness information in the Yahoo Health web page at **http://www.yahoo.com/Health** and at **http://www.yahoo.com/Health/Fitness**.

HAVING A BABY ➤ *pp. 118-119*

Visit the City University of New York's NOAH web site at **http://noah.cuny.edu/** for information useful to pregnant women and their partners.

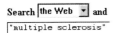

DEALING WITH OTHER
MEDICAL ISSUES ➤ *pp. 119-121*

Use the Alta Vista search service (**http://altavista.digital.com**) to find information about other medical problems or conditions. Chapter 4 describes how to use the Alta Vista search service in detail.

Browsing the Web—in and of itself—won't improve your health. But the Web does provide loads of information that can help you make healthier life choices. Armed with this knowledge, you can live longer and enjoy life more.

GETTING GENERAL HEALTH AND FITNESS INFORMATION

Probably the best places to look for general fitness information and somewhere that you'll always want to include in your explorations are the Yahoo Health web page at **http://www.yahoo.com/Health** and the Fitness web page at **http://www.yahoo.com/Health/Fitness**. There's a bunch of great information here on all sorts of topics.

HOW TO QUIT SMOKING

I quit smoking about 15 years ago. One afternoon, while on the way to the store to buy a cigar, it dawned on me that I was physically addicted to a poison that would ultimately kill me and probably some of the people I loved. I turned around, went home, and never smoked again.

I'm not sure that you can experience the same catharsis merely by browsing the Web. But you may. For starters, take a look at the BADvertising Institute's parody of tobacco advertisements at **http://world.std.com/~batteryb/posters.html**. You'll view tobacco use and its advertising in a whole new haze after seeing posters showing Merit's newest crush-proof box as a coffin, Camel's Joe Cool pictured as the grim reaper, and a tin of Copenhagen snuff containing a photograph of one 27-year-old's cancerous lips and gums. (The poor kid later had his jaw amputated and ultimately died.)

If you're interested in getting information of a slightly less gruesome although still very valuable nature, visit the Ashtray web site at **http://web.bu.edu:80/COHIS/smoking/smoke.htm** (see Figure 8.1). Operated by Boston University Medical Center's Community Outreach

habits & strategies

*Another quitting smoking web directory is maintained by a student, Blair Price, at York University in Ontario, Canada. Price's web page is at **http:// ourworld.compuserve.com/ homepages/bwprice/linkstoa.htm.***

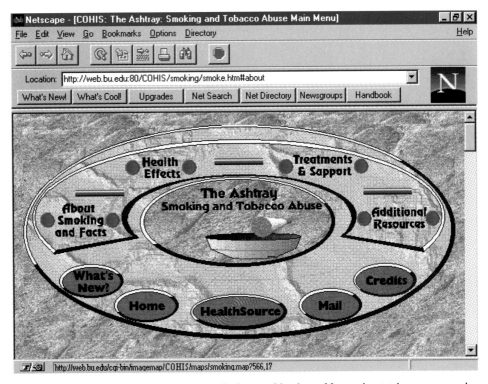

Figure 8.1 Boston University's Ashtray web site provides lots of facts about tobacco use and its health effects

Health Information System, this site provides information about the effects of smoking and other tobacco abuse, including such tidbits as the facts that 1.5 million smokers quit each year (so you can, too) and that smoking is the single most preventable cause of death and disease in the United States. The site also provides ideas about how to quit smoking.

Before I move on to the next health topic, I want to say something especially to any teenagers reading this. In addition to all the other reasons for not smoking—like the facts that smoking makes you sick, makes you stink, and will ultimately kill you—you should know that by smoking you're also giving up an easy route to riches. No kidding. If instead of smoking you stash your cigarette money away in a prudent long-term investment—like a stock mutual fund—you'll amass an easy $1,000,000 by the time you retire.

If you have the time and the inclination, I'd suggest you use a search service such as Alta Vista (described in Chapter 4) to search for web sites or pages addressing alcoholism. You'll get a list of hundreds of web sites and pages.

*The FDA's web site also provides an excellent online magazine. To view a directory that lists recent issues, enter the URL **http://www.fda.gov/fdac** into the Location box.*

DEALING WITH ALCOHOL ABUSE

Some studies suggest that 15 million Americans suffer from alcoholism and that almost 30 million American children grow up in families plagued by alcoholism. So it's no surprise that there's a large volume of information available on the Web about alcoholism.

If you're wrestling with or recovering from an alcohol problem, visit the Alcoholics Anonymous web site at **http://www.alcoholics-anonymous.org/**. This web site isn't in itself a treatment or recovery tool. But it does describe in rich detail the Alcoholics Anonymous programs, traditions, and philosophy.

If someone in your family has a drinking problem or is an alcoholic, take the time to visit the Al-Anon/Alateen web site at **http://solar. rtd.utk.edu/~al-anon/**. Al-Anon provides anonymous, self-help programs for families and friends of alcoholics. Alateen is the sister program that helps teenagers. The Al-Anon/Alateen web site describes these programs.

NUTRITION AND WEIGHT LOSS

If you use a search service like Alta Vista and search on terms like "nutrition" or "losing weight," you'll find thousands of web sites or pages. Unfortunately, many of these sites advertise products and dieting schemes of dubious value. (Although, as an aside, I have to tell you that when I did this, the first match I got was a web page providing the old joke about the man who wants to lose weight and ultimately ends up being chased around his house by a gorilla.) For this reason, your best bet is to start with the U.S. Food and Drug Administration's Center for Food Safety & Applied Nutrition at **http://vm.cfsan.fda.gov/ list.html**. This site documents and describes nutrition problems and risks as well as common dieting and weight loss strategies (see Figure 8.2). You may also want to visit **http://vegweb.com**. (One of the editors working on this book loves this site.)

The only other Internet resource I'll mention is the FatFree mailing list. You can view a web page of back issues of the mailing list at **http://www.fatfree.com/back-issues/**. It's pretty homey stuff, but generally quite good. Mailing list subscribers pass around lots of very-

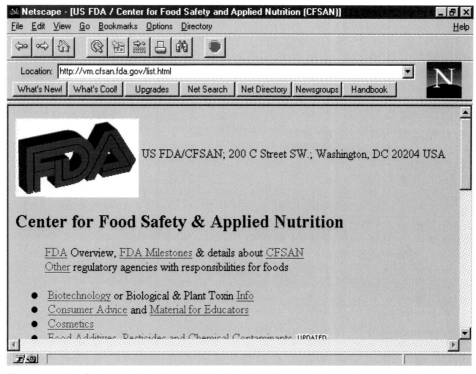

US FDA/CFSAN; 200 C Street SW.; Washington, DC 20204 USA

Center for Food Safety & Applied Nutrition

FDA Overview, FDA Milestones & details about CFSAN
Other regulatory agencies with responsibilities for foods

- Biotechnology or Biological & Plant Toxin Info
- Consumer Advice and Material for Educators
- Cosmetics
- Food Additives, Pesticides and Chemical Contaminants UPDATED

Figure 8.2 The Center for Food Safety & Applied Nutrition provides web pages that document and describe nutrition risks and problems as well as weight loss

low-fat recipes and quite a bit of back-and-forth banter about dietary fat intake. Finally, note that you can usually get subscription instructions to the FatFree mailing list by scrolling to the end of a web page.

PHYSICAL FITNESS AND EXERCISE

As I stated at the beginning of the chapter, probably the best places to look for general fitness information are the Yahoo Health web page at **http://www.yahoo.com/Health** and the Fitness web page at **http://www.yahoo.com/Health/Fitness**. There are hyperlinks to some great information here (see Figure 8.3).

If you are getting ready to start an exercise program, take a peek at the University of Texas–Houston Medical School web page

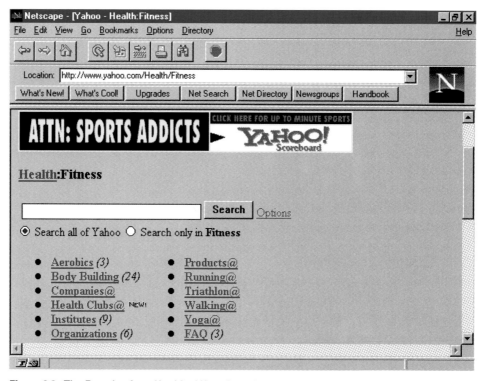

Figure 8.3 The Exercise for a Healthy Lifestyle web page provides some useful information to people wanting to start a new exercise program

at **http://medic.med.uth.tmc.edu/ptnt/00000387.htm**. It provides brief but useful information describing how to start and enjoy an exercise program.

Finally, if you're a woman or you're married to one or you have a daughter, you might be interested in the Women's Line web site at **http://womensline.com/physical/physical.htm**. It provides hyperlinks to numerous web pages and sites dealing with women's fitness and sports issues.

HAVING A BABY

Several hospitals and medical centers provide web sites with information about pregnancy and childbirth. The University of Iowa supports a great virtual hospital at **http://vh.radiology.uiowa.edu/Patients/IowaHealthBook/OBGyn/Pregnancy.html**. The City University of

The NOAH web site pages are available both in English and in Spanish.

New York supports another great site, NOAH, at **http://noah.cuny.edu/** (see Figure 8.4). I particularly like the NOAH site because it tends to address both sides of controversial health issues. If you look up something like abortion at the NOAH site, for example, you'll get information about abortion and hyperlinks to other web pages that present both the pro-life and the pro-choice viewpoints.

SPECIAL MEDICAL PROBLEMS AND CONDITIONS

If you or someone you care about has a special medical problem, you can almost certainly find information about the condition on the Web. Just use one of the search services—I recommend Alta Vista

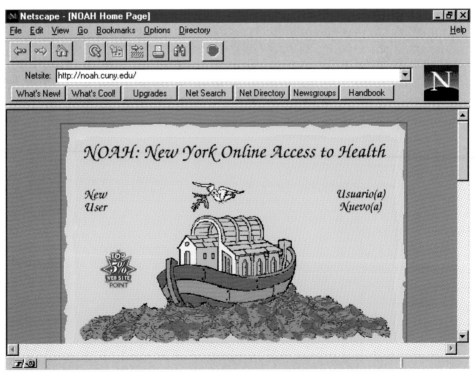

Figure 8.4 The NOAH web site discusses pregnancy and numerous other medical issues as well

(**http://altavista.digital.com**)—and use the name of the medical problem or condition as the search term: multiple sclerosis, HIV, cancer, heart disease, and so on. You'll get numerous hits (see Figure 8.5).

All in all, I think the ability to get information about a particular medical condition or problem that you or someone you care about suffers from is really therapeutic. Hearing about and even corresponding with other people who have experienced or are experiencing what you are is comforting.

Nevertheless, I want to caution you about something. You need to be really careful about getting medical information from, for example, a web page, newsgroup, or mailing list. It's one thing if you're reading an article about, say, prostrate cancer from the University of Michigan's Medical School web site. But remember that one of the features of the Internet is that anyone can say just about anything. And that's true even if the person is a quack, a charlatan, or even just a plain old idiot. So

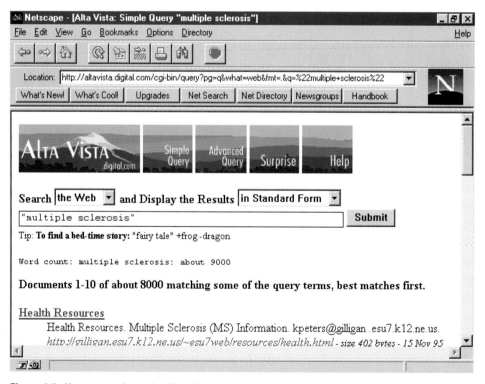

Figure 8.5 Use a search service like Alta Vista to locate web sites or pages that provide information about a particular medical problem or condition

you'll find people talking about miracle drugs that for some, undisclosed reason no major pharmaceutical company wants to sell (yeah, right), Grecian cancer clinics with 90 percent cure rates, and weight loss programs that cure even the most serious case of obesity with herbal therapy. Please be careful. And please, please, please don't use the Internet as a substitute for professional medical care, attention, or consultation. The life you save may be your own.

ON FROM HERE

This chapter and the last one address serious issues such as your money and your health. In the next chapter, you can take a break from such gravity—we'll review the Web resources available to help you have fun.

Travel and Entertainment with the Web

Reservations

FAST FORWARD

PLAN TRAVEL ➤ *pp. 125-128*

Use the Yahoo travel directory at **http://www.yahoo.com/Recreation/Travel/** to get information about a variety of travel-related web pages, but call your travel agent for tickets and reservations—you'll almost certainly get a better deal.

HAVE FUN AND PLAY GAMES ➤ *pp. 129-130*

Use the Yahoo entertainment directory at **http://www.yahoo.com/Entertainment/** to get hyperlinks to thousands of entertainment web pages. Or visit Gid's Games at **http://www.blueberry.co.uk/PIER-Gid.html**—which some people say is the best web games site in the world.

ENJOY THE ARTS ➤ *p. 130*

Use the Yahoo arts directory at **http://www.yahoo.com/Arts/** to get hyperlinks to hundreds of arts-related and museum web sites. Be forewarned, however, that you'll spend forever downloading graphic images.

Newsgroups

MONITOR YOUR CHILDREN ➤ *pp. 131-132*

Be aware that your children can access information when you use the Internet that you may not want them to view. Consider getting filtering software or, better yet, talk with your kids about what they'll encounter and warn them away from the bad stuff.

I should probably start this chapter with a frank admission. While the Web is a pretty neat tool, it isn't going to replace your television set, a good book, or your favorite game. Only the most devoted wirehead is going to want to spend hours browsing the Web just for the pure, unadulterated pleasure of it. Most people, however, can use the Web as a tool for planning some real fun. And that's the tack I'll take here. Along the way, I'll also point out some of the dangers that lurk beneath the surface of some web sites.

PLANNING TRAVEL

Your best bet for good, solid travel information will be through the Yahoo travel directory at **http://www.yahoo.com/Recreation/Travel/**. If you're looking for information about a specific location, click the Regional hyperlink; click the Country, Region, or U.S. State hyperlink; and then click the country, region, or U.S. state you're interested in. If you then choose a country—Figure 9.1 shows the directory listing for France, for example—you get a listing of travel-related web sites for the selected country: activities, lodging, and so forth.

For lodging, the first web site you may want to visit is the All Hotels on the Web site at **http://www.all-hotels.com/**. It lists more than 8,000 hotels around the world. You may also want to visit the TravelASSIST web site at **http://www.travelassist.com/**. It provides web page listings for bed-and-breakfast places, small hotels, and inns. Don't, however, use the TravelASSIST web site as your only information source for lodging. For many areas outside the United States and Canada, it's just not complete enough. (At this writing, there were fewer than 1,000 listings worldwide.)

You can buy airplane tickets using the PCTravel web site at **http://www.pctravel.com/**. It lets you view possible itineraries and fares and even book your flight. (You would typically pay with a credit

CAUTION

There often are regional directories of hotel listings you can use, too. However, my experience is that these tend to list only the most expensive accommodations—and not the inexpensive, mom-and-pop places that can save you money.

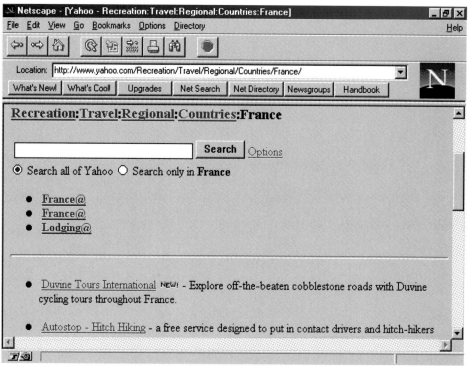

Figure 9.1 The Yahoo web site directory provides a great way to get listings of travel-related web sites organized by country, region, or U.S. state

habits & strategies

The Budget Travel Planning Guide web site at **http://www. travelynx.com**. *is maintained by a travel agency and provides lots of good information.*

card.) I tried the PCTravel web site for a business trip I was planning, but it didn't work very well. Therefore, I don't recommend it. When I requested tickets for a specific date, for example, it indicated the seats were available on flights that were, in fact, full. (My understanding is that the system would have kicked out a cancellation notice a day or so later.) The price per ticket they quoted was around $1,200, even though my travel agent was able to book tickets for around $800. And then, weirdly enough, although the PCTravel web site apparently uses the United Airlines Apollo reservations and ticketing system, it didn't present flights on United, though they were available and were more desirable to me (because I'm a member of United's frequent flier program). I feel kind of bad that I can't recommend PCTravel or some other web-based ticketing system, but I've got to be honest: I think

The web site

http://www.webflyer.com/

maintains an online electronic

magazine devoted to frequent

flyers. If you (like

me) want to

maximize the

benefits of those

free miles you

accrue, visit

this site.

you'll usually do much better with a good travel agent if you need help picking an airline or saving money.

If you don't need help picking an airline or saving money—say you already know which airline you want to fly or which is cheapest—you may want to visit the airline's web site. More and more of the airlines' web sites let you make reservations and purchase tickets online. I already know, for example, that Alaska Airlines almost always has the best deal for me when I fly from Seattle to San Diego (something I do several times a year), so I can book my flight using their web site (see Figure 9.2). If you can't guess an airline's URL, use a search service like Yahoo. Chapter 4 describes how you use search services like Yahoo.

As another option, you can go to the work of making your reservations yourself (via telephone) and then purchase the ticket from a travel wholesaler, Travel Discounters. They have their own web site at **http://www.traveldiscounters.com/** that explains how this works

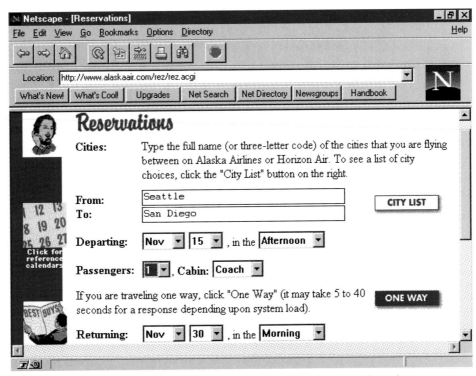

Figure 9.2 The Alaska Airlines web site lets you schedule an itinerary and purchase airplane tickets

Airlines are making small steps toward low airfares on the Web. American Airlines, for example, sells some cheap, weekend flights—called NetSAAver fares— from its site, **http://www.amrcorp.com/ aa_home/.** *Restrictions apply.*

for purchasing tickets at discounts of 17 percent to 30 percent. Note that you need to find the lowest fare and make your reservation, so you're not really getting something for free; you're saving money by doing much of the work yourself. And I didn't actually try this myself. I was pretty fed up with the whole online ticketing experience after trying to make reservations for the aforementioned business trip.

One final note regarding the use of the Internet for planning travel: while I really don't like newsgroups because they waste time, travel planning is the one activity for which the newsgroups may make good sense. If you check out the appropriate rec.travel newsgroups, you may be able to find neat information about visiting a particular location. One easy way to do this is with the **http://dejanews.com/** web site. The Deja News web site, shown in Figure 9.3, lets you specify which newsgroups you want to search—such as the rec.travel newsgroups— and then displays a list of articles matching your search criteria.

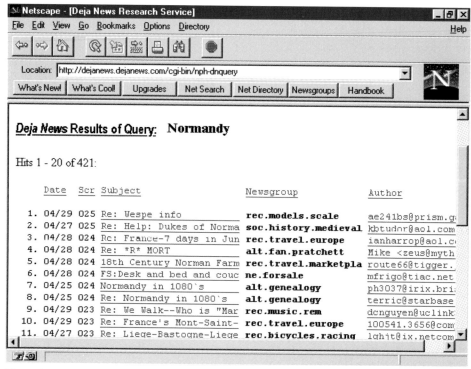

Figure 9.3 Use the Deja News web site to display a list of travel-related newsgroup articles

VISITING THE WEB'S ENTERTAINMENT SITES

The Web provides numerous entertainment-related web sites. If you're interested in fooling around (and don't mind wasting some time on frivolity), first visit the Yahoo web site at the **http://www.yahoo.com/ Entertainment/** directory. It lists a huge, constantly changing, eclectic, and sometimes mediocre set of entertainment-related web sites: event information, archives of jokes (some good, some bad), web-based fiction, online quizzes, gambling web sites (also know as "virtual casinos"), and the list goes on and on and on.

If you like computer-based games, go to the Yahoo directory page at **http://www.yahoo.com/Recreation/Games/Internet_Games/Interactive_Web_Games**. As the URL suggests, it lists a whole slew of interactive web-based games. Figure 9.4, for example, shows a web

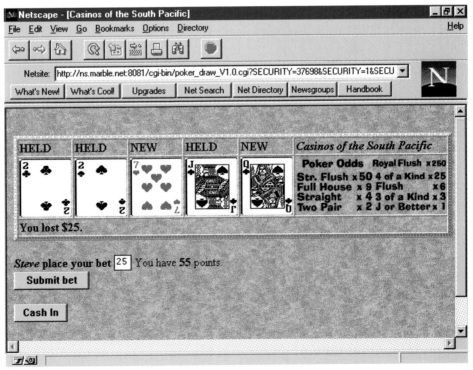

Figure 9.4 Online casinos let you play games of chance

page from an online poker game I was losing when I should have been writing this chapter.

By the way, one games web site you may want to visit is Gid's Games at **http://www.blueberry.co.uk/PIER-Gid.html**. Some people say it's the best web games site in the world.

REVELING IN THE ARTS

The Yahoo web site **http://www.yahoo.com/Arts** provides a directory listing arts-related web sites and pages, too. There are web sites and pages that provide information about everything from architecture and art history to photography and sculpture. (For some reason, the paranormal phenomena web pages also get listed in this directory. But I don't think that's because this stuff is simply entertaining. I mean, it's all real, right?) Figure 9.5 shows the web site for the Art Institute of Chicago.

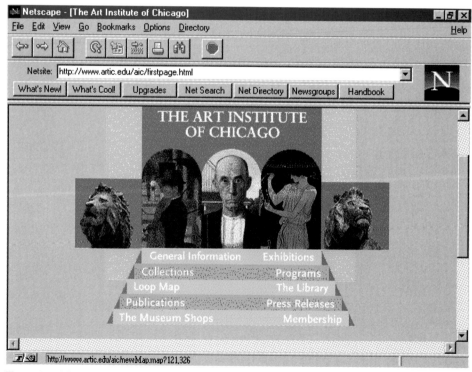

Figure 9.5 Many museums, including the Art Institute of Chicago, have web sites that show off their collections

MONITORING YOUR KIDS

I have mixed feelings about the problems that the Internet presents for parents. Fundamentally, the Internet makes it really easy for people (including your kids) to gain access to all sorts of information. Some of that information is really accurate and useful. Some isn't. Some of that information agrees with your personal values. And some of it doesn't. I believe that this access to information is good.

That much said, however, I want to alert you that there is a dark side to the Internet. This shouldn't be a surprise to you, but in any group of several million people, there are more than a few weirdos. And these weirdos can and do use the Internet's resources and services to move information around the world and to communicate. So no matter how open your mind or liberal your views, you'll find newsgroups, mailing lists, and web sites with content that offends you. And that means your kids will also stumble across content that offends you (although not necessarily them). But therein lies the rub: your kids will be able to get information on all sorts of stuff that you may not want them reading or viewing. Your teenage son will be able to acquire graphic images of people having sex. Your daughter will be able to get information about using or acquiring illegal drugs. And any kid who knows how to click a hyperlink will stumble upon religious or philosophical views that diametrically oppose yours.

You've got two basic approaches for dealing with this reality. One approach is to attempt to physically prevent your kids from viewing this content. If you want to take this tack, there are programs—such as SurfWatcher (web site: **http://www.SurfWatch.com/**) or CyberPatrol (web site: **http://www.CyperPatrol.com**)—that let you block objectionable content. Order either of these from your local computer store or from one of the mail order places. You can also do things like control access to the personal computer. For example, you can put the family's home computer in the family room.

I want to tell you, however, that the "limit physical access" approach is impractical. For one thing, the censor programs can filter content that you don't want filtered. A while back, for example, my local newspaper reported that the White House web site had been filtered because it used the word "couple." At the White House web site, the word was used to refer to the president and his wife. But because the word can also be used to describe sexual intercourse, the censor program filtered the page.

The other problem is that these programs won't filter everything you want filtered. You may be able to prevent kids from visiting the *Playboy* magazine web site, for example. But that doesn't prevent Junior's friend from e-mailing him a message with a picture of Miss December embedded in the message—or handing him a disk with this stuff on it. And there will undoubtedly be other web sites that don't get filtered, even though you find their content objectionable.

The other approach—and this is the one I plan to use with my daughters—is to talk candidly with them, warn them about the riffraff they'll almost surely encounter, and then use this whole issue of objectionable content as just another opportunity for them to mature. My attitude is that they'll soon enough be making these decisions on their own anyway. I'd like to use the Web's ucky side as an opportunity to teach.

ON FROM HERE

Believe it or not, this chapter really wraps up the main portion of this book. You now know not only a bunch of stuff about the Web, you also know how to accomplish real-life work (or play) with the Web. Even so, there are a handful of topics you may want to consider exploring, if you have time. Chapter 10, for example, describes how to solve some common technical problems.

CHAPTER 10

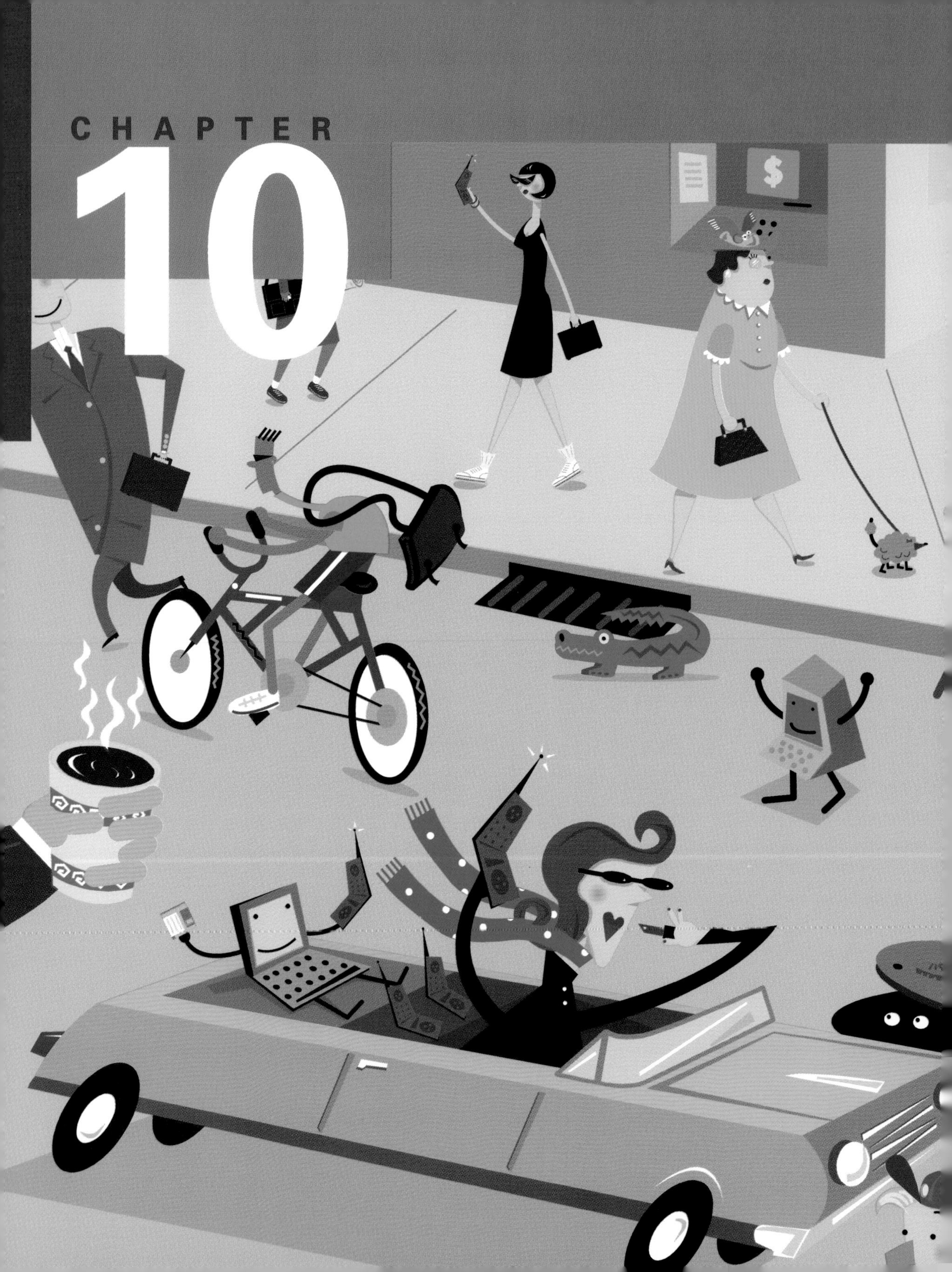

Troubleshooting the Web

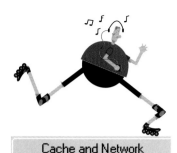

FAST FORWARD

Cache and Network

Search

IMPROVING TRANSMISSION SPEEDS ➤ *pp. 137-142*

To improve the speed with which you browse the Web, don't unnecessarily load a home page you never read; consider browsing only the textual portions of pages; and fine-tune the document cache. You should also get a fast (28.8 Kbps) modem and upgrade to Windows 95 if you haven't already.

BROWSING TOUGH-TO-CONNECT-TO WEB SERVERS ➤ *pp. 142-144*

If you can't connect to a web server, check to make sure you've actually connected. Verify the URL, making sure you haven't used commas in place of periods, or backslashes in place of slashes. If necessary, attempt to connect to the web server's home page rather than the page you want. Finally, consider the possibility that the web server no longer exists.

IMPROVING THE APPEARANCE OF GRAPHICAL IMAGES ➤ *p. 144*

Improve the appearance of the graphical images you view in web pages by adjusting the Windows 95 Display Properties settings to a higher resolution—preferably High Color or True Color.

FIXING BROKEN GRAPHICAL IMAGES ➤ *pp. 144-145*

To fix broken graphical images appearing in a web page, simply reload the page.

PREVENTING VIRUS INFECTIONS ➤ *pp. 145-146*

To prevent your computer from being infected by a computer virus, acquire and install antivirus software such as McAfee's VirusScan.

The Web isn't difficult to use. You probably know that. Nevertheless, there are some common problems you'll encounter. So in this quick chapter, I'll talk about these common problems—and give you some tips for solving them.

TRANSMISSION TIMES ARE SLOW

Let's start with the slow transmission time problem first. It's the big problem with the Web—unless you've got a fast local area network through which you're making your connection. Fortunately, you have several options for addressing this annoyance.

No-Brainer Optimization Techniques

Netscape initially uses the **http://home.netscape.com/** URL as your home page. But unless you're really spending time reading that page every single time you start Netscape, you should change your home page.

If there's some other page you want to always or almost always view, for example, you may make that your home page. (Do make sure that whatever web page you choose as your home page is one that is usually accessible.) Or, you can tell Netscape that it shouldn't load a web. To make such changes, choose the Options|Preferences command and click the Styles tab. The Styles tab of the Preferences dialog box appears (see Figure 10.1). Use the Start With area's Home Page Location text box to provide the URL of the web page you want to use as your home page. If you don't want to automatically load a web page, mark the Start With Blank Page option button.

You can also tweak the way that Netscape runs in order to increase the speed with which you browse web pages. Perhaps the easiest thing to do—and I usually work this way—is not to load the graphical images that pepper most pages. This probably makes sense to you. It might be very typical to have a 50K web page with 90 percent of its content represented by graphical images and only 10 percent of

Other Netscape browser versions and other browsers (like Internet Explorer) also let you make this change, though differently. For example, in Netscape version 2.x you choose Options|General Preferences and click the Appearance tab.

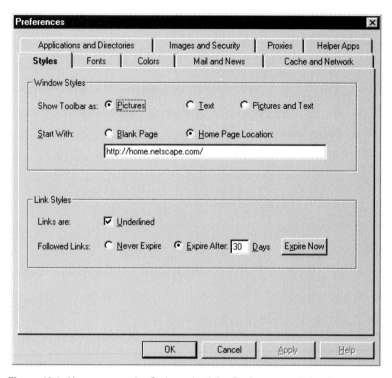

Figure 10.1 You can use the Styles tab of the Preferences dialog box to change the home page Netscape automatically loads every time you start Netscape

If automatic loading of images is turned off, Netscape removes the check mark from the Options|Auto Load Images command. When automatic loading is turned on—by choosing the command again— Netscape places a check mark by the command name.

its content represented by the text you're reading. What this means, obviously, is that of the time you're sitting there twiddling your thumbs, 90 percent stems from the graphical content you're downloading. Sometimes, it's that graphical content you want to view. And in that case, of course, you want to take the time to grab this information. Other times, however, the graphical content is only fluff—simply frosting on the cake. And in those situations, it makes sense to tell Netscape to grab only the textual information.

To do this, turn off the Options|Auto Load Images command by deselecting it. From this point on, Netscape won't automatically load the graphical content of a page. Compare Figures 10.2 and 10.3 to see how the same page looks with and without graphical images. Sure, I admit Figure 10.3 looks a lot nicer, but I'll tell you what: the web page

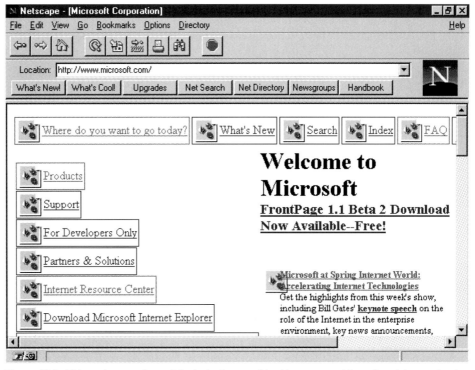

Figure 10.2 This web page doesn't include the graphical images, and therefore takes a short time to display

shown in Figure 10.2 loads in a small fraction of the time that the web page shown in Figure 10.3 does.

If you want to view the graphics associated with a web page, even though you've turned off the automatic loading of images to save time, just choose the View|Load Images command. Netscape loads the graphics along with the text.

There's one final adjustment you can make to improve the speed with which Netscape displays web pages. You can increase the size of the cache. This sounds complicated, but let me explain. If you repeatedly view some web pages—and the web pages don't change between viewing—you actually end up retrieving the same web page information multiple times. And that's silly, because repeatedly moving that same 50K document from some distant web site to your computer is a waste of time. What you should do—and this is probably obvious to you

Figure 10.3 This web does include the graphics, and therefore takes a long time to display

now—is hang on to a copy of the web page by storing it on your computer. Then, what you do is grab this copy from your hard disk (which Netscape can do very quickly), rather than grabbing the web page from its usual web site.

This technique is called *caching*. Netscape is already set up to cache, but you can fine-tune the way it works. To do this, choose the Options|Preferences command. When Netscape displays the Preferences dialog box, click the Cache And Network tab (see Figure 10.4). (In Netscape version 2.*x*, you choose the Options|Network Preferences command and click the Cache tab.) Then use the Cache settings to fine-tune the cache. For example, you can increase the size of the memory cache and the disk cache by increasing the values in the Memory Cache and Disk Cache text boxes. (This will mean that you cache more web pages.) You can also use the Verify Documents option

Other versions of the Netscape browser and other browsers (such as Microsoft's Internet Explorer) also let you adjust the way web pages are cached, although the mechanics work differently.

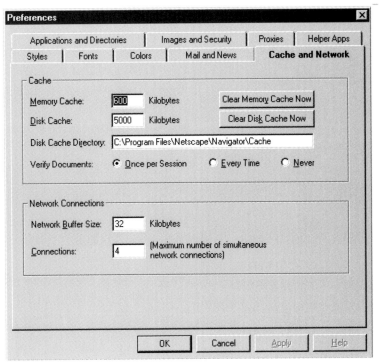

Figure 10.4 The Cache And Network tab of the Preferences dialog box lets you control the way Netscape's caching works

buttons to specify how often Netscape retrieves updated copies of a web page from the original web site.

Willing to Spend Money on the Problem?

If you're willing to spend a bit of money to address the slow transmission time problem, there are two more things you can do. If you're using an IBM compatible, upgrade to Windows 95. No, I'm not suggesting this because I want to help Microsoft sell even more copies. I'm suggesting it because Windows 3.1 and DOS are incapable of transmitting data at high speeds. The problem has to do with the way the modem interrupts the microprocessor to tell it that more data has arrived. I know upgrading to Windows 95 costs money. And maybe you

CAUTION

Because of technical limitations, Windows 3.1 and DOS aren't really capable of transmitting data at 28.8 Kbps. So it probably doesn't make sense to spend more on a fast modem that you'll never be able to operate at top speed.

don't have the $80 or so it'll take. But toy with this idea next time you're redoing your family or departmental budget. You'll get a big payoff in performance.

Here's something else you should consider if you're willing to spend some money on the problem. If you have Windows 95 running on your PC or you're using a Macintosh, you should probably consider getting a 28.8 Kbps modem. That's the fastest modem available. It'll cost you slightly less than $200 at this writing. But assuming you're running Windows 95 or a Macintosh, you'll move data around at twice the speed possible with a slower 14.4 Kbps modem.

Just for the record, I don't think that an ISDN modem, or digital modem, is all that great, even though it transmits data at two to four times the speed of a regular 28.8 Kbps modem. ISDN modems are often a real bear to get working right. And ISDN service is often very expensive. So I wouldn't even waste time exploring this option unless you've got a local friend or associate who's already connected to the Internet using ISDN service and who can explain to you exactly how you make this connection and how much it costs. (By the way, you also need to make sure that this friend uses the same local telephone company as you do.)

YOU CAN'T CONNECT TO A WEB SITE

If you can't connect to some web site, your problem is usually one of three things: a bad or lost connection, a bad URL, or a problematic web server. Most problems are easy to address.

Verify the Connection

Your first task is to make sure you're still connected to the Web. You can do this by displaying the Dial Up Networking window, as shown in Figure 10.5. If it shows you're connected, then you are. If it doesn't, you aren't, and you'll need to reestablish your connection. (You can do this by clicking the Reconnect button, which will appear on the Dial Up Networking window if you've lost your connection.)

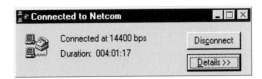

Figure 10.5 The Dial Up Networking window shows whether you're connected

Double-Check the URL

It's easy to goof up the URL—especially for beginners. So if you can't connect to a web site and you've already verified that you haven't lost your dial-up networking connection, double-check the URL's spelling. Make sure the periods really are periods and not commas. And make sure the slashes are slashes and not backslashes.

If this checking still doesn't provide a clean URL that results in a web page being loaded, another thing you can try is simplifying the URL so you land at the web site's home page and then use its hyperlinks to move to the web page you actually want to view. For example, suppose you want to view the web page described with the following URL:

http://home.netscape.com/newsref/pr/index.html

If you had trouble entering this URL in the Netsite box, you could instead just enter the web site name described with the following and much simpler URL:

http://home.netscape.com/

Then you could move from this web site's home page to the specific page you want by clicking hyperlinks. No, it's not a perfect solution. And it does require a bit more work. But if you're having trouble with a particular URL and can't get it to work any other way, you'll sometimes find this technique quite useful.

If you know the connection is working and you're pretty confident about the URL, you should also consider the possibility that the web site is either shut down—perhaps for routine maintenance—or that the web site is too busy. In either case, your best bet is to wait a few minutes and try again. And if that doesn't work, you may want to try some other day.

Netscape will replace any commas you type with periods, but other web browsers may not be so forgiving.

One final comment: Don't waste too much time trying to connect to some problematic web server. It's possible that the web server has either moved (and changed its URL) or that it no longer exists. Not surprisingly, I looked at hundreds and hundreds of web sites (maybe even thousands) as part of writing this book. And I saw a bunch of web sites come and go. (Unfortunately, a few of the web sites I mention in this book probably no longer exist by the time you read this.)

YOUR GRAPHICAL IMAGES DON'T LOOK SHARP

If the graphical images that you're seeing on your screen don't look at least as sharp as those shown in the pages of this book, you need to adjust your display settings. In Windows 95, you can do this by right-clicking the Windows 95 desktop (the area behind the program windows), and then choosing the Properties command.

When Windows 95 displays the Display Properties dialog box, click the Settings tab to display the Settings options, as shown in Figure 10.6. Then use the Color Palette drop-down list box to increase the number of colors to as rich a color set as you can. True Color (24-bit) is best. High Color (16-bit) is still pretty good. 256 color will often look sort of gritty if you're displaying photographic images. And 16 color usually looks pretty crummy. While you're making these changes, see if you can use the Desktop Area slider button to increase the resolution, too.

FIXING BROKEN GRAPHICAL IMAGES

Sometimes the graphics in a web page won't load correctly. When this happens, Netscape displays a broken picture icon (see Figure 10.7).

CAUTION

If you boost your Color Palette setting too high for your monitor, you won't be able to see anything. If this happens, restart your computer. When you see the message "Starting Windows 95," press F8, choose Safe Mode, and reduce the setting.

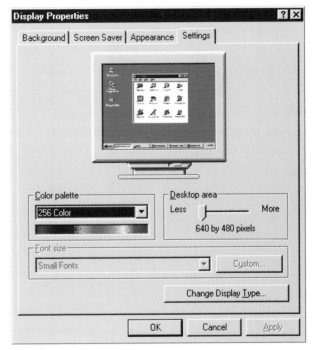

Figure 10.6 In Windows 95, the Settings tab of the Display Properties dialog box lets you adjust the color palette and resolution of your design

Fortunately, these broken graphical images are easy to fix. Just click the Reload icon on the toolbar, or choose the View|Load Images command. Easy, right?

PREVENTING VIRUS INFECTIONS

It's possible—although unlikely—that your computer will catch a virus from a file you download. Viruses can be nasty things, but contrary to what you read in the newspaper or hear from some television

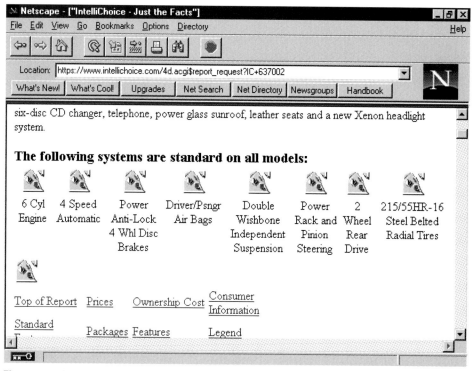

Figure 10.7 When Netscape can't load the graphics in a web page, it displays broken picture icons in place of the image

*Antivirus software usually costs
between $50 and $60.*

newsperson, you're quite unlikely to catch one. I've only had my computer attacked by a computer virus once. (A coworker's son infected his laptop by sharing games with the kids at school and then almost infected the computers in our office.)

Nevertheless, if you're going to regularly download files from the Web—and you're not particularly choosy about the servers you connect to—you may want to get and use antivirus software. You can get product information about the F-Prot Professional antivirus from **http://www.datafellows.fi/f-prot.htm** web site and about the McAfee VirusScan antivirus from the **http://www.mcafee.com/** web site. You can order antivirus software from any computer store or mail order place.

ON FROM HERE

Where you go from here (at least in terms of your future reading of this book) is hard to predict. Chapter 11 provides a quick-and-dirty primer on how to start publishing stuff on the Web. (I'll even give you the bird's-eye view of HTML, the language used to create web pages.) Finally, the last three chapters, Chapters 12, 13, and 14, point out some neat web sites for businesses, adults, and kids.

CHAPTER 11

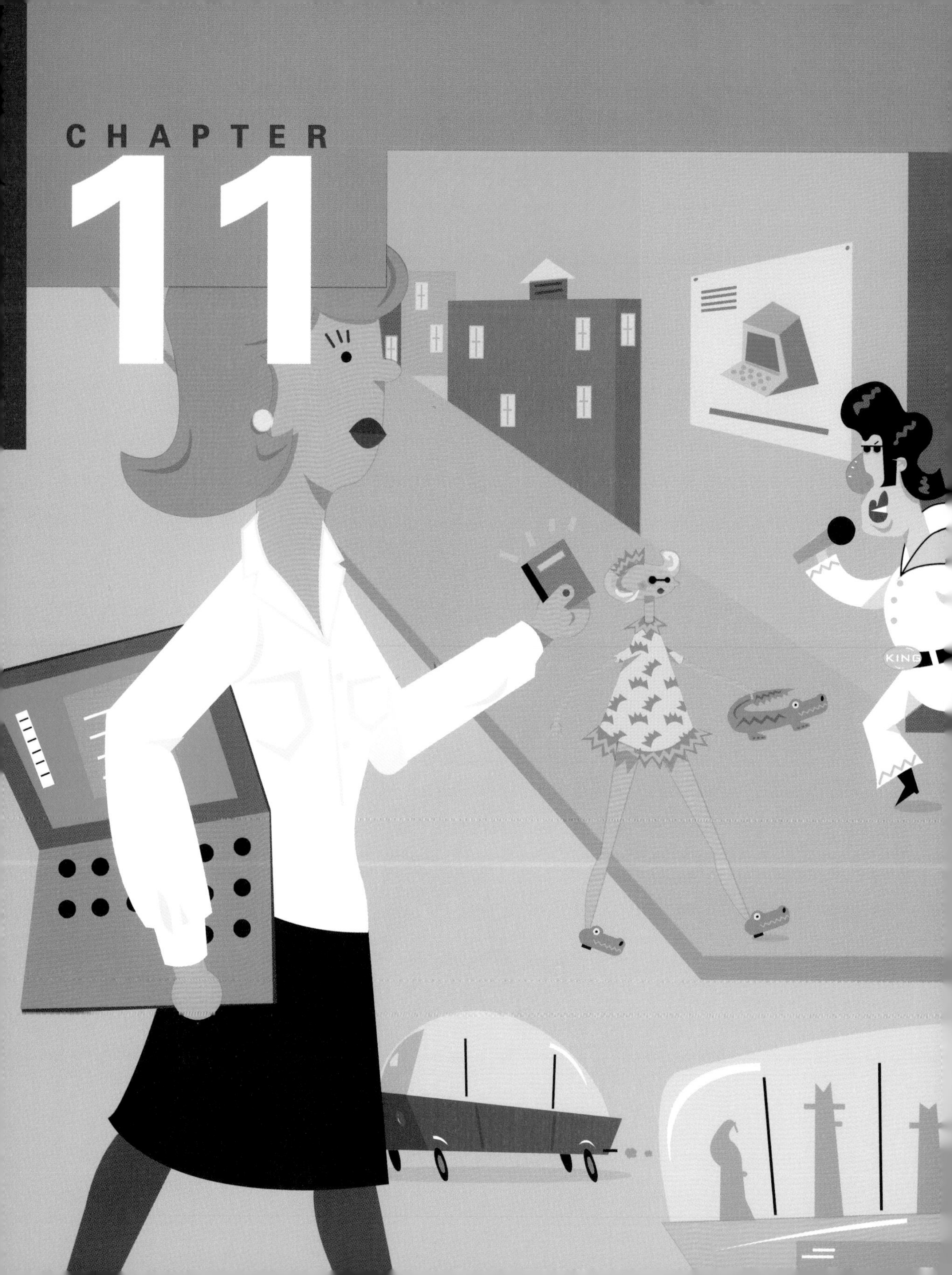

Web Publishing Basics

FAST FORWARD

```
<h1>Roadmaps to Wealth</h1>
<body>
```

INTRANET SOLUTIONS

ADD URL

WEB PUBLISHING RATIONALE ➤ *pp. 151-156*

Internet web publishing works well as an advertising medium, a distribution channel, and a component of a product or service. *Intranet* web publishing works well as an internal-to-an-organization communication tool.

DEVELOPING CONTENT ➤ *p. 157*

Developing the content you want to publish on the Web is the first step. Figure that a web page—excluding video, audio, or Java or JavaScript applications—requires about the same amount of effort as a page of a magazine, book, or brochure.

CREATING HTML DOCUMENTS ➤ *pp. 157-161*

You can create HTML documents by hand-coding the different elements of a web page, but you need to know HTML. Most web publishers will find it much easier to use an HTML editor or a program that has a built-in HTML editor.

SETTING UP A WEB SERVER ➤ *pp. 161-163*

If you don't mind spending $10,000 to $20,000 to start, you can set up your own web server. But it's more economical to rent either disk space or a server from an Internet service provider who specializes in helping web publishers.

PROMOTING YOUR WEB SITE ➤ *pp. 163-165*

Once you set up your web site, you'll want to promote it by adding your new web site address to popular web directories, your business cards, and letterhead. You may also want to publicize your new web site in brochures and through newsgroup posting and mailing list messages. You may even be able to get other web publishers to promote your site.

This chapter's discussion is pretty general, but I do assume that you've at least perused the material in Chapters 1, 2, and 3.

All the earlier chapters of this book talk about how you use the Web as a tool for getting your work done or how you use the Web as a toy to have fun. But this chapter takes a different approach. It discusses how you use the Web as a tool to communicate with customers, employees, and other groups. I am not, by the way, going to bog you down with a bunch of details. This is big-picture stuff. What we're going to do here is talk about why you publish on the Web, how you publish on the Web, and how you promote your web site once it's done.

WHY PUBLISH ON THE WEB?

Why publish on the Web? It's a really good question. Unfortunately, I'm not sure there's any one answer. Some people use the Web as an advertising medium. Some as a distribution channel. And some—and this is really most clever—use the Web as a component of their product or service. A person could write a whole book on these subjects alone—and I'm sure someone will—but it probably will be helpful to just quickly review the reasons and ways in which firms publish on the Web.

The Web as an Advertising Medium

Not surprisingly, many web publishers view the Web simply as an advertising medium. And for some businesses it works wonderfully well this way. For example—and don't be offended by this—if you look at what *Penthouse* or *Playboy* magazine does (**http://www.penthousemag.com** or **http://www.playboy.com**), you have to admit that they probably build demand for their products by providing little snippets from the magazine via the Web (see Figure 11.1). People read the online magazine (or look at the pictures) and then decide to pick up a copy of the print magazine. And that's one traditional way to use the Web as a product advertising medium.

habits & strategies

As a rule, the best commercial web sites are those that some company has decided to spend a lot of money on, in essence as a form of institutional advertising. The Microsoft Corporation web site, for example, falls into this category.

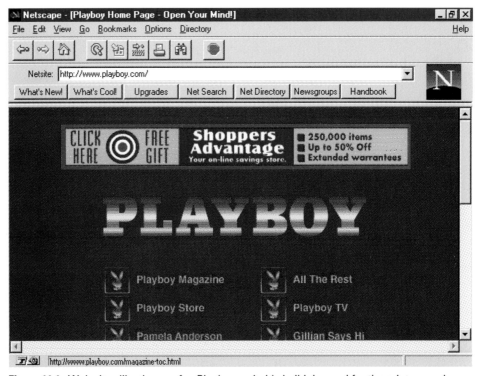

Figure 11.1 Web sites like the one for *Playboy* probably build demand for the print magazine

Creating demand isn't the only approach to advertising, however. Many firms successfully use the Web as a way to provide detailed product information. Look at the web sites of any of the direct-mail computer manufacturers—Micron Technology at **http://www.micron.com** (see Figure 11.2) or Gateway 2000 Computers at **http://www.gw2k.com**, for example. You'll see that they use their web sites to provide prospective customers with voluminous quantities of technical product information: microprocessor clock speeds, megabytes of memory or disk space, graphic card capabilities, and so on. This works really well. Customers can easily check specifications and prices—and at just about any hour of the day or night.

I don't want to sound like Simple Simon here, but note, too, that using the Web in either of these ways delivers two big advantages as compared with traditional print-based advertising. You don't pay any

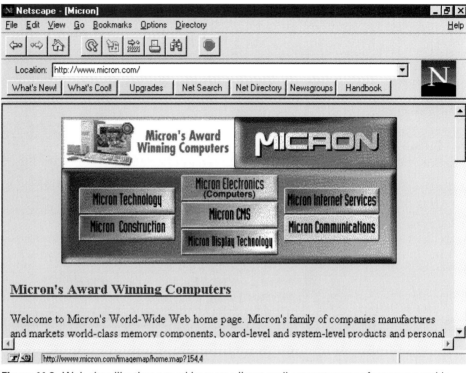

Figure 11.2 Web sites like those used by many direct-mail computer manufacturers provide detailed product information

The cost to write or develop, edit, and then design web pages should roughly equal the cost to write or develop, edit, and then design a page of printed matter.

printing costs (only the relatively cheap costs of maintaining or renting a web server). And you don't wait for several weeks or several months for the printing and possibly publication of your advertisement. To publish your web pages, you just move them to the web server.

The Web as a Distribution Channel

Some firms use the Web as a distribution channel. I think this works best for firms selling products that are already digital—in other words, stored as a file on a disk. Netscape does this, for example. Whenever Netscape releases a new version of some piece of software—which is by definition a digital product—it makes the software available on its web and FTP servers. Registered users, or *subscribers,* as they're called, then visit the web site and download the new program files (see Figure 11.3).

Figure 11.3 Netscape Communications Corporation uses its web site both to advertise and distribute its products

With a 28.8 Kbps modem, it takes about five minutes to move a megabyte of stuff from some web server to your computer's hard disk.

Other firms can digitize their products (by converting them into files that can be stored on disk) and then use the Internet to move these files from creator to customer. This represents another angle on using the Web as a distribution tool. It's not a terrible idea, I guess. And you see lots of newspapers and magazines following this route. But I'll make a fearless prediction about this group. Few people will make money, because a computer monitor's pictures and text—even a very good monitor's—lack quality compared with printed matter and cause more eyestrain; because a book or magazine is more portable than a PC; and because simply transferring content from print media (like a magazine or book) doesn't provide the reader with anything new.

The Web as a Component of a Product or Service

One of the smartest reasons to become a web publisher is to enhance your current product or service, or to improve some important business function like customer support. Obviously, not every business can reengineer part of their operation to take advantage of the Web in this way. And, to be quite honest, only a handful of companies have really done a good job of this so far. But the opportunities are enormous. For example, explore the United Parcel Service web site at **http://www.ups.com/**. Sure, it does the usual web page stuff like advertising (see Figure 11.4). But it also lets UPS customers request package pickups and track packages. It's pretty cool stuff.

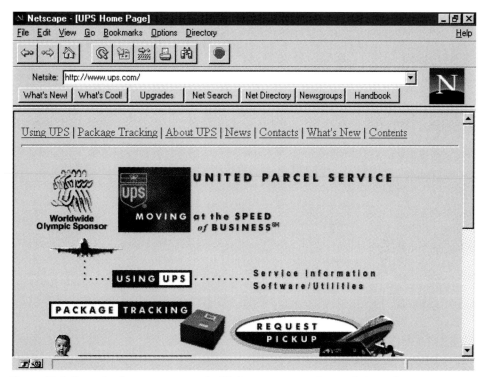

Figure 11.4 Some businesses can use the Web as a way to enhance their product or service—as United Parcel Service did

To publish a sophisticated intranet web (or Internet web!), use web authoring software such as Adobe PageMill or Microsoft's FrontPage. (There are other such programs, but PageMill and FrontPage usually get good reviews.)

The Web and Intranets

Okay, here's another idea you may not have thought of. It's very easy to build an internal web, or *intranet,* on just about any network: Novell NetWare, UNIX, Windows NT, or you name it. If your business already has a computer network, all you have to do is create web pages and then store them on some easily accessibly network file server. Once you've done this, anybody with a networked personal computer and a web browser can easily browse the web pages.

An intranet gives organizations—particularly large organizations—an economical yet powerful way to communicate with employees. Publishing something like an employee handbook on an intranet, for example, should make it easy (or at least easier) to keep such a document up-to-date. And hopefully it would also make the document easier to use. A pregnant user interested in maternity leave information could search on the term "maternity."

And Then There's the Really Big Money

Over the last few weeks, I've been reading a book about Western Europe during the 14th, 15th, and 16th centuries. What continues to intrigue me about this period is how a new technology—moveable type for printing presses—affected the world in unpredictable and sometimes scary ways. The Protestant reformation (and the ensuing political and religious turmoil). The creation of national languages and literature. The translation and dissemination of Arabic and Greek scientific knowledge. The list goes on.

I'm not a philosopher, economist, or political pundit. I just write books about using computers. But I'll still suggest to you that the Internet and especially the Web (because it's so easy to use and so powerful for sharing information) will affect the world in more ways than I've described here. It won't just be an advertising medium or distribution channel. People will figure out how to use web publishing in other powerful and profitable ways. And if you're one of the people who realizes this and figures out some clever new way to exploit the technology, there's no telling what you may be able to do.

HOW TO CREATE AND PUBLISH YOUR OWN WEB PAGES

There are three elements to creating and publishing your own web pages: developing the content, creating the HTML documents, and placing the HTML documents on a web server. I'm not going to bore you to death with a bunch of minutiae, but if you're seriously considering web publishing, you'll truly benefit from an overview of this process. So that's what I'll do here.

Developing Content

The very first thing you need to do is develop information, or *content* as it's called, that you want to share by using a web page. While this may sound pretty easy, it's not. Creating any substantial content requires a lot of work. It can take a few days, for example, to write a good, 1,000-word article. Writing an online, 50,000-word book can take several weeks or months. A single illustration can take an hour or two. And don't even get me started on the work required to create good audio content, video clips, or Java-based applications. I'm not going to beat this drum any longer, but the place to start a successful web publishing project is with good content—a rule that most neophytes ignore.

Creating HTML Documents

HTML is a crummy little language that tells a web browser how to display text, pictures, and other objects in a web page, and which web page to jump to when a hyperlink gets clicked. You can actually create an HTML document using your word processor. All you do is enter HTML instructions into the document. The document is just a text file. Figure 11.5 shows an example HTML document. Figure 11.6 shows how this web document looks when viewed with a web browser.

The first line uses the code **<html>** and the last line uses the code **</html>** to identify the document as one that uses HTML instructions. You'll notice that HTML codes come in pairs. There will always be a beginning tag (**<html>** in this example) and a terminating tag (**</html>** in this example).

Java is the Web's de facto programming language. In essence, Java and its little brother, JavaScript, let your web browser run programs stored on or retrieved from a web server.

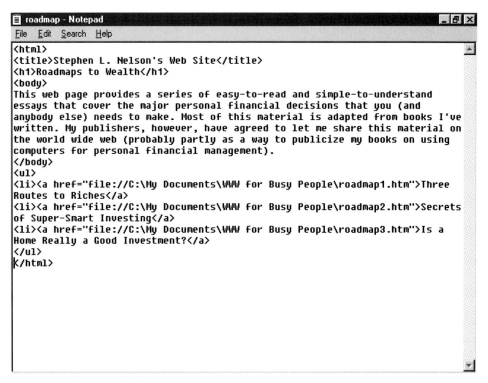

```
roadmap - Notepad                                              _ B X
File  Edit  Search  Help
<html>
<title>Stephen L. Nelson's Web Site</title>
<h1>Roadmaps to Wealth</h1>
<body>
This web page provides a series of easy-to-read and simple-to-understand
essays that cover the major personal financial decisions that you (and
anybody else) needs to make. Most of this material is adapted from books I've
written. My publishers, however, have agreed to let me share this material on
the world wide web (probably partly as a way to publicize my books on using
computers for personal financial management).
</body>
<ul>
<li><a href="file://C:\My Documents\WWW for Busy People\roadmap1.htm">Three
Routes to Riches</a>
<li><a href="file://C:\My Documents\WWW for Busy People\roadmap2.htm">Secrets
of Super-Smart Investing</a>
<li><a href="file://C:\My Documents\WWW for Busy People\roadmap3.htm">Is a
Home Really a Good Investment?</a>
</ul>
</html>
```

Figure 11.5 This is an HTML document

The second line names the web page:

```
<title>Stephen L. Nelson's Web Site</title>
```

See how this works? You enter the code **<title>** at the start of the line. Then you enter the actual title text. Then you enter the code **</title>** at the end of the line. Notice that this title appears on the title bar of the web browser window (see Figure 11.6).

The third line puts the "Roadmaps to Wealth" heading at the top of the page:

```
<h1>Roadmaps to Wealth</h1>
```

Again, how this works is pretty obvious. You just enclose the heading within the HTML codes **<h1>** and **</h1>**.

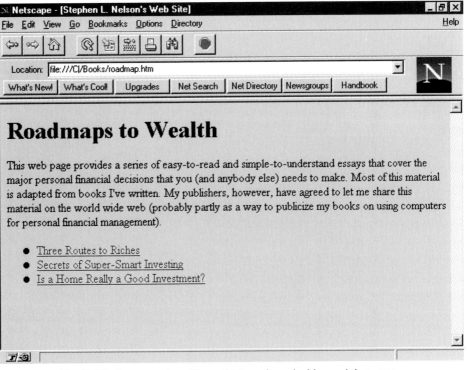

Figure 11.6 The HTML document from Figure 11.5 as viewed with a web browser

habits & strategies

The spacing and line breaks in your HTML don't affect the way your document looks when viewed with a web browser. The HTML codes control that sort of stuff.

Following the heading is the main body of text you see in Figure 11.6. Mostly—and as you might expect—this is just the text you want people to see on your web page. The only trick is that you need to begin the text with the **<body>** code and end it with the **</body>** code. In Figure 11.5, I put these codes on separate lines, but you wouldn't have to.

The rest of the HTML document, shown next, is only slightly more complicated:

```
<ul>
<li><a href="file://C:\My Documents\WWW for Busy
People\roadmap1.htm">Three Routes to Riches</a>
<li><a href="file://C:\My Documents\WWW for Busy
People\roadmap2.htm">Secrets of Super-Smart
Investing</a>
<li><a href="file://C:\My Documents\WWW for Busy
```

*If you use Microsoft Word 7.0,
you can get a free copy of the
Internet Assistant for Word from
the Microsoft web site
(http//www.microsoft.com). It's
reported that Word 8.0 and later
will easily create, save, and
open HTML documents.*

```
People\roadmap3.htm">Is a Home Really a Good
Investment?</a>
</ul>
```

The **<ul>** and **</ul>** codes that appear on the first and last lines of the preceding block of text tell your web browser that what's enclosed in them is an unnumbered list.

The lines that begin with the **<li>** code are the actual hyperlinks. The **<li>** code just tells your web browser to display a bullet, or dot (see Figure 11.6). The remaining information on each of these lines represents the hyperlink. For example, on the first hyperlink line, the portion of the instruction

```
<a href="file://C:\My Documents\WWW for Busy
People\roadmap1.htm">
```

tells the web browser to move to a file stored on my C hard drive. You probably aren't used to seeing a URL look this way, but that's exactly what it is. If I instead wanted someone to move to the Microsoft Corporation home page when clicking this hyperlink, I could edit this portion of the instruction to read as follows:

```
<a href="http://www.microsoft.com">
```

Do you see how this works? The actual URL just gets enclosed in the quotation marks.

The last part of the hyperlink is the text you'll use for the clickable text:

```
Three Routes to Riches</a>
```

The remaining three hyperlink instructions look and work basically the same way. There's an HTML code that tells the web browser to display a bullet. There's the portion of the HTML instructions that provides the URL. And, finally, there's the portion of the instructions that provides the clickable text someone sees in the web browser window.

You now understand the basics of HTML. But let me quickly tell you three other things. First of all, you shouldn't have to fool around with the actual HTML codes. If you get web authoring software, you would only import, say, a Word document and then click toolbar buttons and choose commands to assign HTML formatting.

Second, there's a lot more that you can do with HTML than I've show here. You can add graphics, tables, downloadable files, and so on.

Third, unless you possess good design skills, the web pages you create probably aren't going to look very good. In fact, they may even look like the one shown in Figure 11.6. Ugh.

Setting up a Web Server

Once you've got your HTML documents finished, all you need to do is stick them on a web server. If you want the web pages to be available to anyone browsing the Internet's web, of course, you send the web pages via FTP to a web server that's connected to the Internet. But there are actually a couple of ways you can do this. You can set up your own web server, for example. Or you can just rent a few megabytes of disk space on somebody else's web server.

The Expensive Web Server Option

Setting up your web server requires the most work and the most money. To set up your own web server, for example, you'll need one or more computers to function as servers. (Figure they'll cost a few thousand dollars each.) You'll need web server software—and that may cost you anywhere from a few hundred dollars to a few thousand dollars. Finally, you'll need to lease a special, superfast connection to the Internet, such as a T1 line. (You can also sometimes rent part of a T1 line or share a T1 line with someone.) All totaled—and rounded to the nearest thousand dollars—you're probably looking at around $15,000 to start and then maybe another $2,000 a month. And these amounts don't include the costs of paying some UNIX or Windows NT guru to manage your web server. (That could easily run another $60,000 a year.)

If you want to go this route, ask your computer systems administrator to get the ball rolling. Unless he or she's been in a cave for the last year or two, he or she's going to know people who know people.

habits & strategies

If you want the web pages to be available as an intranet to network users within your organization, place the web pages on a web server that's accessible to anyone working on the network.

A T1 line passes data at the speed of 1.5 Mbps (megabits per second). That's more than 50 times as fast as a 28.8 Kbps (kilobits per second) modem.

The Renter Option

The renter option is easier and cheaper. All you need to do is find someone who will let you store your web pages on their web server. If you already have an Internet service provider, for example, they will probably let you do this. America Online lets its subscribers store up to 2 megabytes of web pages on its web servers. GNN, a popular Internet service provider owned by America Online, lets its subscribers store up to 20 megabytes of web pages on its web servers. These services have different pricing options—and the pricing seems to change regularly—but you're probably looking at a monthly cost of only $10 to $20. Some Internet service providers even specialize in helping web publishers and provide all sorts of extra services: statistical analysis of your web traffic, web page design, and so forth. (The charges for these services often run a couple hundred bucks a month.)

By the way, there is a potential problem with the space renter option. It's this: some of the people who browse your web site or see your web site's URL will be able to tell that you've gone the cheap, rented-disk-space route. For example, when a URL looks like this:

http://www.aol.com/stevespages

you can tell the web publisher is just renting space on America Online's server, because the *aol.com* is the domain name for America Online. On the other hand, if you saw a URL that looks like this:

http://www.steveswebsite.com/

you might think, "Gee, that Steve...his business must be as big as General Motors if he's got his own web site."

To mitigate this potential image problem, some Internet service providers will help you get your own domain name (such as **steveswebsite.com**), which you can then use as part of your web site URL. And you'll look cooler. Or something. If this whole image thing sounds like an issue you want to explore in more detail, get a recent issue of *Internet World* magazine. Its pages will contain scads of advertisements for Internet service providers who specialize in helping web publishers.

A typical big web page might use 100 kilobytes of disk space, so 2 megabytes of space on a web server should easily let you store up to 20 web pages, and 20 megabytes of space should let you store up to 200 web pages.

PROMOTING YOUR WEB SITE

Okay, say you've gone to the work of developing great content. And say you've already placed your web pages on some server. Is that it? Are you done? Absolutely not. You need to promote your web site so people will know it's there and will visit it. There are several steps you should take.

Step 1: Add Your Web Site to a Directory

Request that your web site be added to Yahoo's directory (**http://www.yahoo.com**) and to any other appropriate directories. To add your web site to the Yahoo directory, visit their web site, click the Add URL hyperlink, and then follow its instructions (see Figure 11.7).

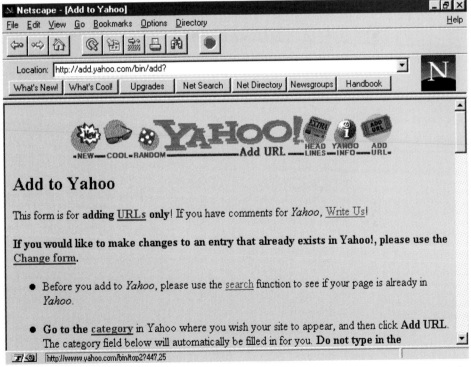

Figure 11.7 Click Yahoo's Add URL hyperlink to get information about adding your web site address to the Yahoo directory

Note that it often takes several weeks for your directory listing to appear. You should also see instructions for adding your web site address to other directories, too.

At this writing, adding a web site to the Yahoo directory is free. Yahoo also provides a service called Yahoo Launch, however, which sticks an advertisement for your new web page on some other, heavily used web page. At one point, I think the web launch service costs about $1,000 a month, although Yahoo says the price will go up as more people browse the Web.

The large search services such as Alta Vista can reportedly index the entire World Wide Web in about a week. This should mean that after your web site address gets added to a popular directory (like Yahoo's), it should start appearing in search service indexes about a week later. If all goes well.

Step 2: Add Your URL to Business Cards, Letterhead, and Brochures

This one is obvious, right? If you think about your web site address in the same way as a telephone number, it belongs on all of your business cards, letterhead, and brochures. If you advertise in other ways, you may also be able to provide your web site address in this manner.

Step 3: Publicize Your Web Site Address in Newsgroup Articles

You need to be careful about this, but say you're an attorney who specializes in family law. And say you regularly visit a newsgroup that deals with family law issues. One of the slickest ways to publicize your web site is to post interesting articles to the newsgroup and include your web site address. In this manner, people who see your stuff, like it, and want to learn more, may visit your web site.

I should warn you that you need to be careful about doing this. Subtlety is key. Using our example of the attorney practicing family law, you don't want to simply post an article that says, "Hey everybody, visit my web site." No way. You want to respond to some other reader's post about how joint custody works, providing good solid informa-

Chapter 5 describes what newsgroups and mailing lists are.

tion—and your URL. Or you want to write a well-thought-out article about how to solve sticky, divorce-related income tax problems and then include your URL. You get the picture.

Step 4: Send Messages to Relevant Mailing Lists

You can also publicize your web site by sending messages to a relevant newsgroup. Again, subtlety is key. Discretion is essential. Everything I just said in the preceding blurb about newsgroups also applies to mailing lists.

Step 5: Collaborate with Other Web Publishers

Many web publishers won't have this option, but sometimes you'll be able to collaborate with other web publishers. Maybe there's some other business that's related to yours but not really a competitor. Maybe you breed horses, for example, and they operate a tack shop. In this situation, the other web publisher may be happy to add your URL to their page if you'll add their URL to your page. It doesn't hurt to ask.

Step 6: Add More Content

One final thing: A general rule of thumb is that you need to keep adding more new, good content in order to keep people coming back for subsequent visits and to keep your web site fresh. This obviously doesn't help you promote your web site to new viewers. But it helps retain existing viewers.

ON FROM HERE

I'm not big on promoting a publisher's other books—even though they like it when you do. However, I do want to mention to you that Osborne/McGraw-Hill publishes another Busy People book that specifically talks about how to publish web pages, *Web Publishing with Netscape for Busy People*. If you want more information about publishing stuff you've created on the Web, you might want to pick up a copy. I've given you an introduction to the web publishing process here, but there are all sorts of other little nuances and subtleties you'll want to know about.

Ten Truly Useful Business Web Sites

INCLUDES

- Web site addresses and profiles for:
  Apple Computer, Microsoft Corporation,
  The Internal Revenue Service, The Library
  of Congress, The CNN Financial Network,
  United Parcel Service, ZDNet, AT&T's Toll-free
  Directory, The All Business Network, and The
  U.S. Business Advisor

FAST FORWARD

IN TODAY'S ISSUE
....
Tax Info For You.

APPLE COMPUTER ➤ *pp. 170-171*
Get information about Apple Computer products from
http://www.apple.com.

MICROSOFT CORPORATION ➤ *pp. 171-172*
Microsoft Corporation maintains one of the best sites there is at
http://www.microsoft.com.

INTERNAL REVENUE SERVICE ➤ *p. 172*
The IRS web site at **http://www.irs.ustreas.gov/prod/**
cover.html is valuable to anyone who files a United States federal
income tax return.

THE LIBRARY OF CONGRESS ➤ *pp. 173-174*
The Library of Congress web site at **http://lcweb.loc.gov** is
complicated, but it's definitely the place to go for government
information and information about books.

THE CNN FINANCIAL NETWORK ➤ *pp. 174-175*
As mentioned in Chapter 7, the CNN Financial Network web site at
http://www.cnnfn.com supplies financial and business
information.

UNITED PARCEL SERVICE ➤ *pp. 175-176*
The United Parcel Service web site at **http://www.ups.com** not
only provides great value to UPS customers, but it also provides a
textbook example of how to create a great business web site.

ZDNET ➤ *pp. 176-177*

The Ziff-Davis Net web site at **http://www.zdnet.com** helps you keep up-to-date on the computer industry and on new computer hardware and software.

AT&T TOLL-FREE INTERNET
DIRECTORY ➤ *pp. 177-178*

On the **http://www.tollfree.att.net/** web page, AT&T provides a search engine that lets you search for 1-800 numbers.

ALL BUSINESS NETWORK ➤ *pp. 178-179*

The All Business Network web site at **http://www.all-biz.com/** amounts to a virtual smorgasbord of useful business resources.

U.S. BUSINESS ADVISOR ➤ *pp. 179-180*

The U.S. Business Advisor web site at **http://www.business.gov/** provides all kinds of federal information for businesses, in a surprisingly easy-to-access format.

In some ways, it's foolish of me to try and pick the ten best business web sites. What I like or am interested in may be completely different from what you like or are interested in. Nevertheless, I did want to tell you about some of the most useful web sites for businesses.

APPLE COMPUTER

Appendix C provides information especially for Apple Mac users who want to browse the World Wide Web.

http://www.apple.com

Want to know more about Apple products or solve some problem you're having with, say, your Apple Mac? Try the Apple Computer home page (see Figure 12.1). It provides detailed product information for all of Apple's software and hardware products, often including a list of

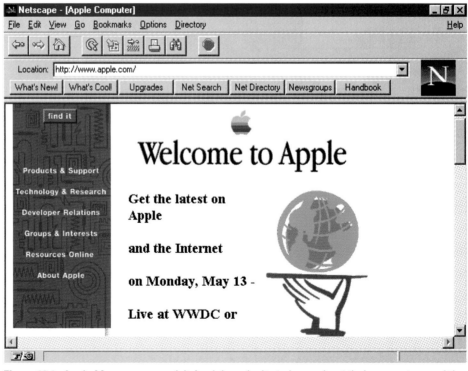

Figure 12.1 Apple Mac users can visit Apple's web site to learn about their computers and the company that sells them

compatible third-party products. The Apple web site also supplies all kinds of help, including a library of technical support information, its *Information Alley* newsmagazine, and instructions about how to call Apple.

If you don't find the Apple Computer information you need on the Apple page, you may still want to start there. From the Apple home page, you can move to many other good Apple-related web pages including Macintosh user group web pages, web sites providing Apple Macintosh freeware and shareware, and web sites describing third-party products that work with Apple computers.

MICROSOFT CORPORATION

http://www.microsoft.com

You may be surprised to hear this, but I think Microsoft's web site is probably the best. The Microsoft web site (see Figure 12.2) provides

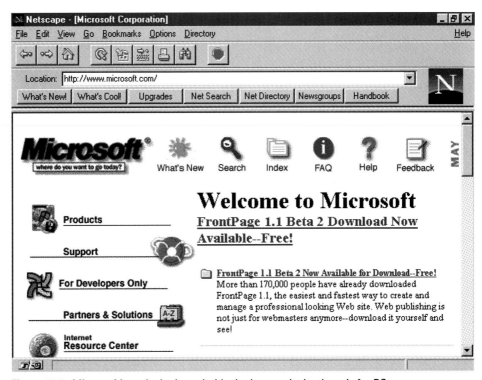

Figure 12.2 Microsoft's web site is probably the best web site there is for PC users

Microsoft Word users can download a free copy of the Internet Assistant for Microsoft Word, an HTML editor that works with Microsoft Word. For more information about HTML, refer to Chapter 11.

just a ton of neat stuff for business computer users. For starters, these pages deliver product and technical support information about all of Microsoft's products—including extensive information about Windows 95, Windows NT, and Microsoft Office. And then there are all those useful files and programs you can download for free, including templates for Microsoft Office, Excel, and Word. You can even download a free copy of Microsoft's web browser, the Internet Explorer.

If you're having a problem with a Microsoft product, you can use the Microsoft Corporation web site to get technical support. Just click the Support hyperlink. Once you get into the Support web pages, by the way, be sure to take the time to explore Microsoft's Knowledge Base database. By using Knowledge Base, you can learn what problems other users have had—and how they solved them.

THE DIGITAL DAILY

http://www.irs.ustreas.gov/prod/cover.html

The IRS' Digital Daily (see Figure 12.3) advertises itself as "faster than a speeding 1040-EZ" and is definitely the quickest help I've ever gotten from the IRS. Perhaps most helpful, this web site lets you search and download tax forms and publications. The IRS provides these forms in several formats, including PostScript, so if you're in a hurry to part with your money (or get your refund), you can just print the forms, fill them out, and send them in. The page also provides online filing information, a list of frequently asked questions, a section summarizing important tax changes, tax information for businesses, and a description of IRS programs and services for small businesses.

Figure 12.3 The best feature of the IRS' web site? It lets you download tax forms

THE LIBRARY OF CONGRESS

http://lcweb.loc.gov

The Library of Congress web site (see Figure 12.4) is complicated, no doubt, but it's definitely the place to go for government information and information about published books. From here, you can search for and display congressional records and House and Senate bills and resolutions. You can also find information and links for hundreds of local, state, federal, and even international government agencies, including a great deal of information from the U.S. Copyright Office. If you're looking for a book, you can also use the Library of Congress site to search for

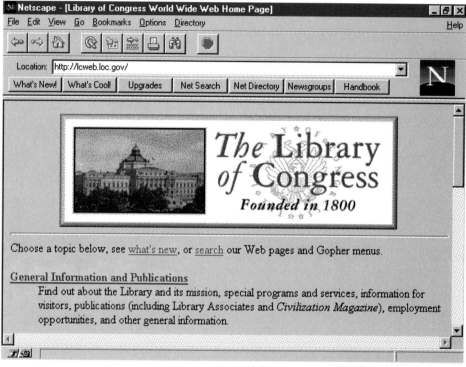

Figure 12.4 The Library of Congress is sort of a mess, but it provides great content

copyrighted works to determine their ISBN numbers, or to find out which U.S. libraries carry them. If you're just browsing, you can also search through a few digital collections, and you can follow numerous Internet links, which are organized by subject.

THE CNN FINANCIAL NETWORK

http://www.cnnfn.com

As mentioned in Chapter 7, the CNN Financial Network page (see Figure 12.5) supplies lots of financial information to help you keep up-to-date, and to find out what's going on in various markets worldwide. On its News page, you'll find business-related articles; included in each article are links to related stories and related WWW sites. Its Markets page has 15-minute-delayed stock quotes, information on the commodities mar-

Figure 12.5 Numerous online news web sites exist, but CNNFN is probably the most useful business news web site

kets, a comparison of the U.S. dollar and other currencies, and world stock market indices. If you like to watch the CNN Financial Network, this page also has a broadcast schedule, show profiles, and transcripts. The site links to many useful WWW pages, including the World Bank, the IRS, temporary agencies online, and resources for small businesses.

*Federal Express provides a similar page at **http://www.fedex.com**.*

UNITED PARCEL SERVICE

http://www.ups.com

If you ship a lot of packages, the UPS page (see Figure 12.6) can make the process a lot easier. Instead of calling for a pickup, if you're sending Next Day Air or 2nd Day Air shipments, you can just send in a request

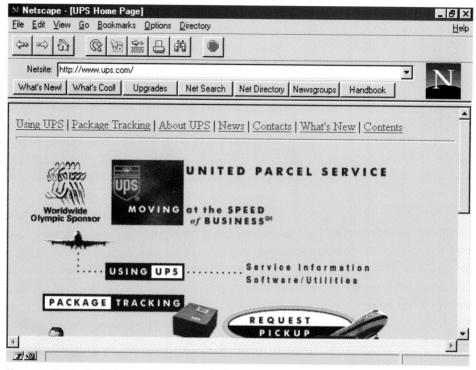

Figure 12.6 The United Parcel Service web site provides useful services for UPS customers, demonstrating how businesses can use the Web as a powerful business tool

from this page. You can also find out how much it will cost to send your package and how many days it will take. And if you've sent a package and you're really nervous about whether it will get there on time—or if it doesn't arrive at all—you can just type in the tracking number and find out where the package is. (You can also download Apple Mac and Windows software that helps you track up to 20 packages at a time.)

ZDNET

http://www.zdnet.com

The Ziff-Davis page (see Figure 12.7) can help you keep up-to-date on the computer industry and on new computer hardware and software. It has quite a few magazines online, including *Mac User*, *MacWeek*, *PC Computing*, *PC Magazine*, and *PCWeek*. Each magazine is available in

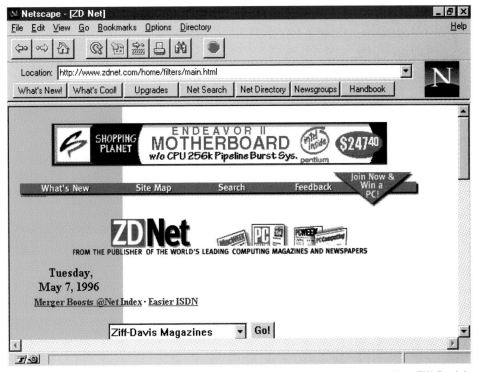

Figure 12.7 The ZDNet web site provides lots of computer-related information from Ziff-Davis' popular computer magazines

a colorful (if busy) format, and you can also search each magazine, or all the magazines, for the topic you're interested in. You can personalize this page to show you only the information you're interested in. The Ziff-Davis page also has a link to Ziff-Davis Labs, which tests hardware and software for performance and compatibility, and then publishes its results.

AT&T TOLL-FREE INTERNET DIRECTORY

http://www.tollfree.att.net

On this page (see Figure 12.8), AT&T provides a search engine that lets you search for 1-800 numbers. In its searches, AT&T lets you enter

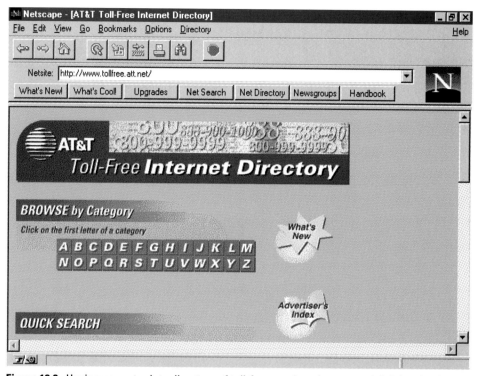

Figure 12.8 Having an up-to-date directory of toll-free numbers is very useful. A few bucks of long-distance savings here, a few bucks there...pretty soon you're talking about real money

information in different fields such as category name, city, and telephone number; and even use Boolean operators and wildcards. If you like, you can also browse by category, clicking on a letter to get a list of categories.

ALL BUSINESS NETWORK

http://www.all-biz.com/

Probably the second most useful business web site, the All Business Network web pages (see Figure 12.9) offer a wide range of useful business resources. This web site supplies articles on various topics and hyperlinks to business-related magazines (which often provide the full text of all their articles), libraries, companies, government agencies,

178

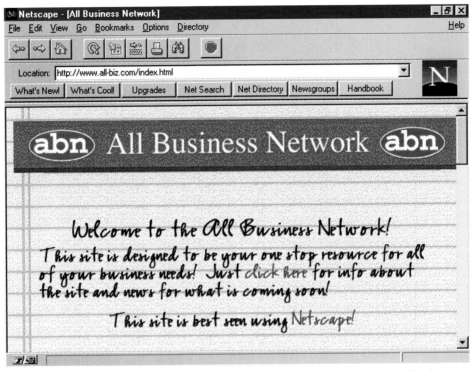

Figure 12.9 The All Business Network web site is probably the second most useful business web site

trade associations, and newsgroups. You can get to these hyperlinks either by going to the main menu or by looking up a specific topic, such as marketing, computers, or transportation. There's also an area for business services, which provides links to resources for many business needs, such as banking, accounting, and legal services. Other handy areas of the All Business Network include its hyperlinks to online business suppliers and shipping companies and its search engine for the Chamber of Commerce.

U.S. BUSINESS ADVISOR

http://www.business.gov/

This government site (see Figure 12.10) provides all kinds of federal information for businesses, in a surprisingly easy-to-access format. If

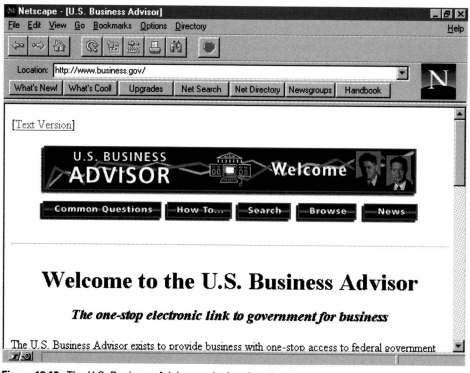

Figure 12.10 The U.S. Business Advisor web site gives businesses access to federal government information and services

you just have a quick question, you can go to a list of commonly asked questions, organized by category. You can also browse or search for resources and information such as small business resources, postal service information, information on how to do business with the government, OSHA publications, the Social Security Handbook, information on laws and regulations, information on  getting loans, and information on where to get free tax help. The U.S. Business Advisor also has a link to FEDWORLD, which lets you access government bulletin boards.

ON FROM HERE

The Web isn't only business, there's lots of fun to be had. The next chapter can help you get in on the fun—it describes ten entertainment web sites.

Ten Cool
Personal Web Sites

FAST FORWARD

1000 Fifth Avenue
New York, New York
10028

THE METROPOLITAN MUSEUM OF ART ➤ *pp. 186-187*

Find out about the Metropolitan Museum of Art, and look through some of its artwork by visiting **http://www.metmuseum.org/**.

THE INTERNET MOVIE DATABASE ➤ *pp. 187-188*

If you're looking for the name of an obscure movie, or you want to know all the movies your favorite actor or actress played in, visit the **http://us.imdb.com/** web site.

USA TODAY ➤ *pp. 188-189*

USA Today provides an online version of its popular national daily newspaper at **http://www.usatoday.com/**.

THE BRANCH MALL ➤ *p. 189*

The Branch Mall at **http://www.branchmall.com** is home to all kinds of companies selling all kinds of products.

Copyright Warning

THE LYRICS PAGE ➤ *p. 190*

Use the Lyrics Page at **http://archive.uwp.edu/pub/music/lyrics** to search for a song based on its composer, title, or lyrics.

BOTANIQUE ➤ *p. 191*

The Botanique web site at **http://www.botanique.com** describes hundreds of botanical gardens in the United States and Canada.

INTERNET RADIO ➤ *p. 192*

The RealAudio web site at **http://www.realaudio.com** supplies free downloadable software that lets you listen to audio over the Internet, and it broadcasts its own online radio station.

BRADFORD ROBOTIC TELESCOPE ➤ *p. 193*

With the Bradford Robotic Telescope at **http://www.telescope.org/rti/**, you can sit in front of your computer and have a robotic telescope in West Yorkshire, England, take pictures for you.

ONLINE NEWSHOUR ➤ *pp. 194-195*

If you like to watch *NewsHour with Jim Lehrer,* but you're short on time, you'll definitely want to check out the Online NewsHour page at **http://web-cr01.pbs.org/newshour/**.

ON-LINE BOOKS ➤ *pp. 195-196*

The On-line Books web pages at **http://www.cs.cmu.edu/Web/books.html** offer more than 1,600 public domain books in HTML format.

Your taste in entertainment and fun may be quite different from mine. But even so, I'd like to be bold and tell you about some of my favorite, just-for-fun web sites. At the very least, by visiting some of these sites, you'll gain additional perspective about what's available on the World Wide Web. And, hopefully, you'll have some fun.

THE METROPOLITAN MUSEUM OF ART

http://www.metmuseum.org/

The Met's web site (see Figure 13.1) gives you a slick way to find out about the Metropolitan Museum of Art and to look through some of its artwork. By clicking on the Collection link, you can get an overview of

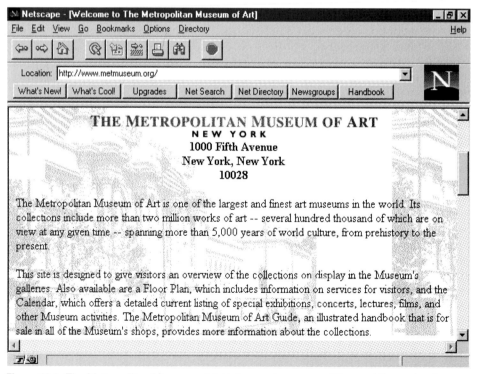

Figure 13.1 The Metropolitan Museum of Art lets you view some of the world's masterpieces

CAUTION

Your computer monitor and graphics card won't do justice to many works of art.

the museum. You can then click on different parts of the museum to select a collection, or you can browse by selecting a subject. Once you've selected a collection, you can look at general information about the collection, or you can look at specific works of art.

The Metropolitan Museum of Art web site also provides a calendar of events, including special programs and exhibitions, travel and dining information, a gift shop from which you can buy products securely (using your credit card), and a news section that describes what's new and upcoming in the galleries.

THE INTERNET MOVIE DATABASE

http://us.imdb.com/

If you're looking for the name of an obscure movie, or you want to know all the movies your favorite actor or actress played in, chances are you'll find the information in the Internet Movie Database (see Figure 13.2). It

Figure 13.2 Looking for a good video to rent? The Internet Movie Database may be just the tool you need

has information on approximately 65,000 movies from all over the world, ranging from early movies (the earliest is from 1898) to cult movies to popular movies. You can search for any of these movies by movie title, cast or crew name, date or location, genre, subject, and keyword. About 8,000 of the movies have been reviewed, and many have information such as cast lists, plot summaries, lists of goofs, and essays. The database also has links to movie clips and links to pictures of stars.

USA TODAY

http://www.usatoday.com/

Lots of newspapers are going online, and they're a good way to find out what's going on without wasting reams of paper. *USA Today* provides a good interface: when you load the home page, you see a colorful page that looks just like the front page of a *USA Today* newspaper (see Figure 13.3). You can click on different parts of the page to get to the News,

Figure 13.3 The web version of *USA Today* is a great way to stay up-to-date on what's happening in the United States and around the world—especially for people who travel overseas

Sports, Money, Life, or Weather sections, and the top two stories of the day. You can even do an online crossword. If you're looking for specific information, you can search the archives for stories in back issues of *USA Today*.

THE BRANCH MALL

http://www.branchmall.com

The Branch Mall (see Figure 13.4) is home to all kinds of companies selling all kinds of products, from ordinary products like perfume, flowers, wine, and computer hardware and software, to exotic products like hot-air balloon rides over Michigan, bumper-sticker poems, and live Maine lobsters. The mall makes it pretty easy to order products—you just fill out a form that describes what you want. To pay, you use a credit card.

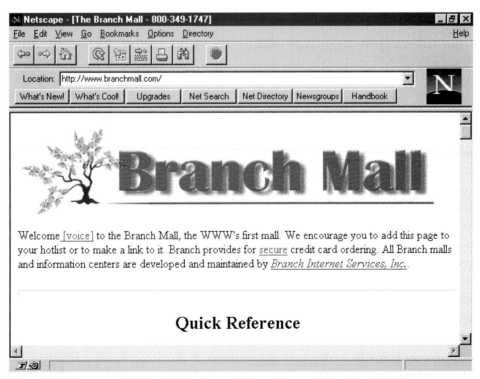

Figure 13.4 If you want to shop but don't want to leave home, try the Branch Mall

THE LYRICS PAGE

http://archive.uwp.edu/pub/music/lyrics

Have you ever forgotten some of the lyrics to your favorite song? Or had a song you couldn't get out of your head, but not known what it was? If so, you might want to try the Lyrics Page (see Figure 13.5). It has lyrics for thousands of songs, and you can search through it by author or title, or by entering words from the body of the song. It found almost all of the songs I looked for, even many obscure songs. But beware: I discovered that if I wasn't careful about what I entered, the search engine brought up tons of songs I didn't want and had never even heard of. And use common sense. Don't search for words like "love" or "car." Keep in mind, too, that most of the songs on this page are copyrighted, so you can't legally post them or otherwise distribute them.

Figure 13.5 Music buffs should have fun with the Lyrics web pages

BOTANIQUE

http://www.botanique.com

Botanique also maintains a calendar of quite a few garden sales and plant shows around the United States.

A site for flower lovers, Botanique (see Figure 13.6) is the jumping-off spot for hundreds of botanical gardens in the United States and Canada. You can click on a map of the United States or Canada, and it will show you all the botanical gardens for each state or province, or by city. Many of the botanical gardens provide information about the garden, maps to the garden, and admissions information. Some of them even provide full-fledged tours, so you can look at some of their best displays and read about some of their more exotic plants.

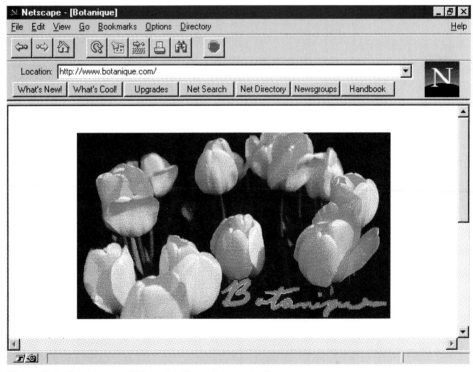

Figure 13.6 Gardeners will love the Botanique web site

CAUTION

The Internet is relatively

slow—bandwidth is limited—

so the reception is

pretty poor. In the

next few years the

Internet should

get faster, and

the audio quality

should improve.

INTERNET RADIO

http://www.realaudio.com

The RealAudio web site (see Figure 13.7) supplies free downloadable software that lets you listen to audio over the Internet, and it broadcasts its own online radio station. In addition, the RealAudio web site supplies hyperlinks to other web sites supporting RealAudio, including NPR, ABC, PBS; various radio stations; numerous Internet sites with live news broadcasts, talk shows, music shows, coverage of sports events and music festivals; a narrated art exhibit; and U.S. Supreme Court oral arguments. Basically, anything that can be put in audio format, you'll probably be able to find through the RealAudio page.

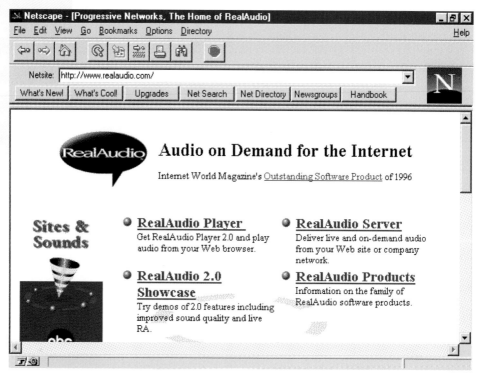

Figure 13.7 The RealAudio web site lets you listen to audio over the Internet—including a radio station that uses the Internet to broadcast

Because of high demand for the

telescope, you might have to

wait several days for your

picture to be taken. Part of the

time you're

waiting, you can

look at 500

pictures taken

by other Internet

users.

BRADFORD ROBOTIC TELESCOPE

http://www.telescope.org/rti/

To practice astronomy, you used to have to go to all the trouble of going outside at night and looking through the telescope. Not anymore. With the Bradford Robotic Telescope, you can sit in front of your computer and have a robotic telescope in West Yorkshire, England, take pictures for you. You send in a request for a picture of a planet, a galaxy, or any section of the night sky. The telescope then puts your request in a queue, depending on the request's priority, and takes the picture as soon as it can. It then sends you an e-mail notifying you that it has taken the picture, and displays the results on the Bradford Robotic Telescope page (see Figure 13.8).

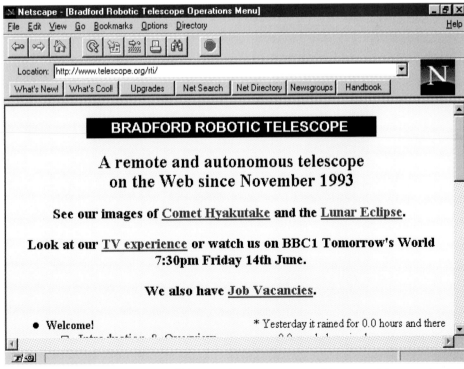

Figure 13.8 The Bradford Robotic Telescope lets you stargaze with your web browser (sort of)

ONLINE NEWSHOUR

http://web-cr01.pbs.org/newshour/

If you like to watch *NewsHour with Jim Lehrer,* but you're short on time, you'll definitely want to check out the Online NewsHour page (see Figure 13.9). It has transcripts from the show, complete with pictures, and it also has some radio segments. If you want more information than you can find in any one transcript, you can also search through an archive of transcripts from old shows, or you can get background information about subjects you want to know more about by going to a section that categorizes past shows by subject, or by clicking on hypertext links within some of the transcripts.

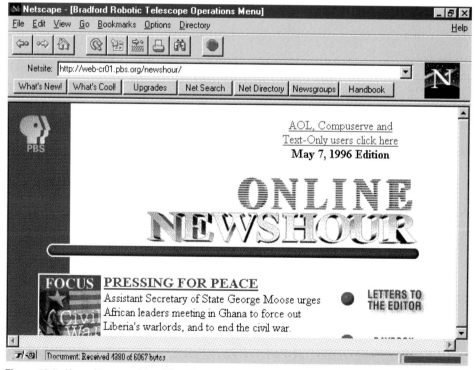

Figure 13.9 If you like watching *NewsHour with Jim Lehrer* but don't have time or don't get home in time, visit the NewsHour web pages

If you're just browsing, you can look at a section of essays on anything from the origins of humans to mystery movies, or you can read dialogues between David Gergen, editor-at-large for *U.S. News and World Reports,* and famous writers and philosophers. You can also ask questions of special guests through the Online NewsHour's Online Forum. The guest reads through all the questions submitted and puts the answers to selected questions on the Online NewsHour page.

ON-LINE BOOKS

Chapter 11 explains what HTML is and how web publishers use it.

http://www.cs.cmu.edu/Web/books.html

The most exciting thing about the World Wide Web for me is that it can store huge amounts of information and let me access it quickly and easily. Right now, a few organizations are taking advantage of that capability by putting thousands of public domain books on the Internet. Out of all these pages, the On-line Books page (see Figure 13.10) is the

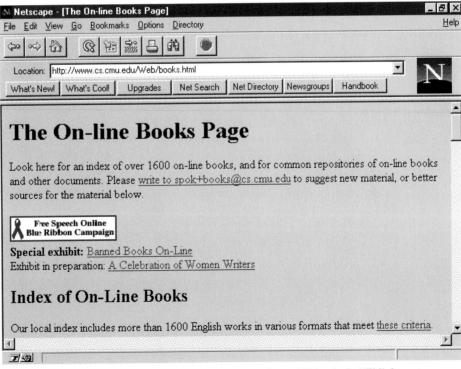

Figure 13.10 The On-line Books web site offers more than 1,600 books in HTML format

nicest and most convenient to browse through. It offers more than 1,600 of these books in HTML format, so they're easy to navigate. You can search the On-line Books page by author or title, or you can just browse through it (although I don't recommend browsing through a list of 2,000 books). If you can't find what you're looking for on the On-line books page, you can also look through a fairly long list of book-related links.

ON FROM HERE

If you've got kids and they have the patience to wait for web pages to load, you might want to peruse Chapter 14. It describes a handful of web sites of interest to young children and their parents.

CHAPTER 14

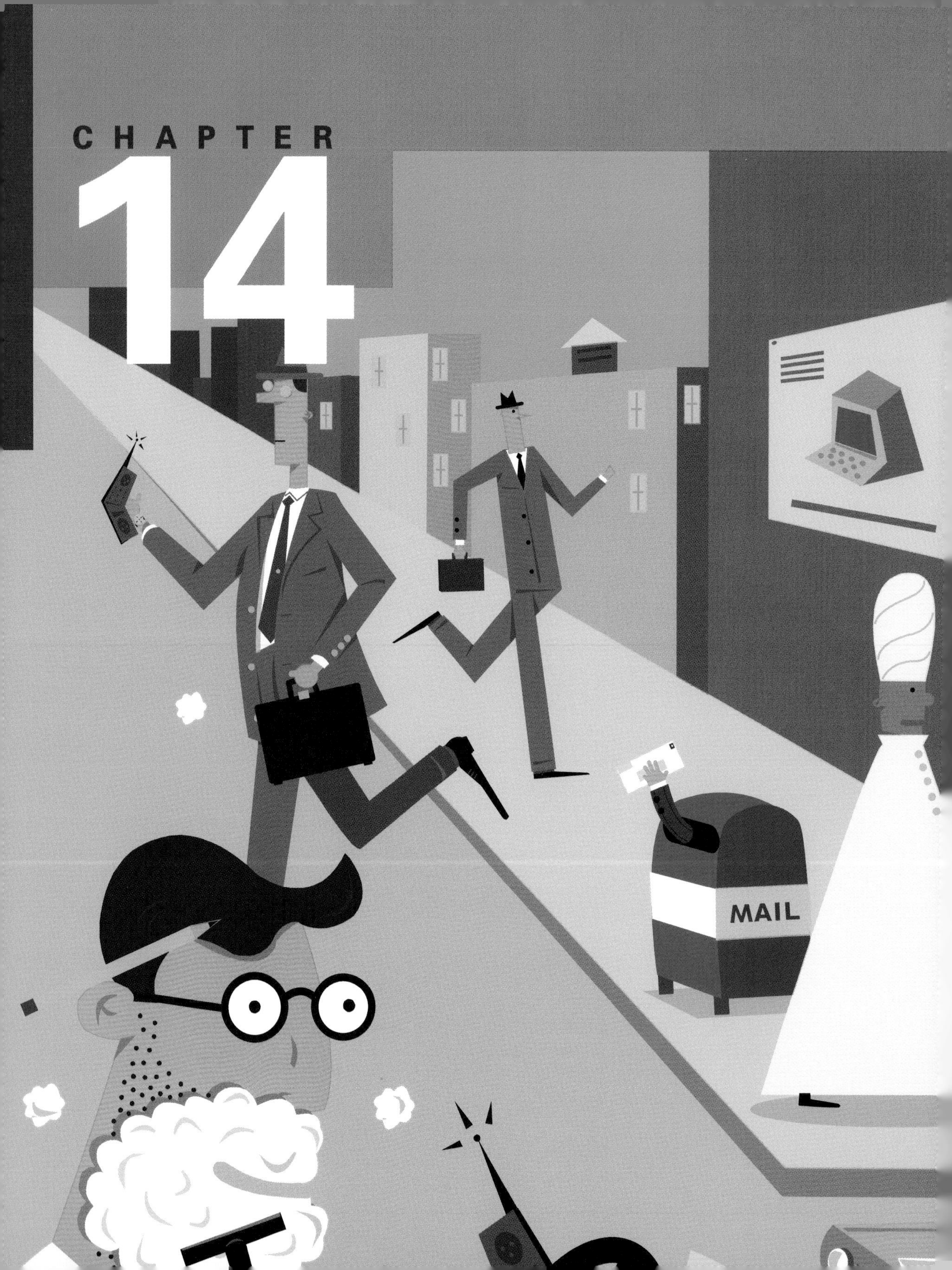

Ten Neat Web Sites for Parents and Kids

FAST FORWARD

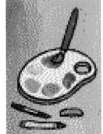

CYBERKIDS ➤ *pp. 202-203*

The CyberKids web site at
http://www.cyberkids.com/index.html is a fun, colorful
magazine for children.

PARENTSPLACE ➤ *pp. 203-204*

ParentsPlace, **http://www.parentsplace.com/**, provides good
information on basic and preventative health care for children.

PARENT SOUP ➤ *pp. 204-205*

Parent Soup, at **http://www.parentsoup.com**, supplies
information on parenting, in a well-designed magazine format.

NATIONAL AERONAUTICS AND
SPACE ADMINISTRATION ➤ *p. 205*

Children interested in space flight or astronomy should visit the
NASA web site (with the help of their parents) at
http://www.nasa.gov.

MISTER ROGERS' NEIGHBORHOOD ➤ *p. 206*

The *Mister Rogers' Neighborhood* web pages at
http://www.pbs.org/rogers target parents and educators,
not children.

DISNEY ➤ *p. 207*

The Disney web site at **http://www.disney.com** provides photos, audio clips, video clips, downloadable icons, and downloadable wallpaper images for many Disney movies.

KID SAFETY ON THE INTERNET ➤ *p. 208*

The University of Oklahoma Department of Public Safety created this fun, easy set of pages for children to browse through to learn basic safety information. Visit it at **http://www.uoknor.edu/oupd/kidsafe/start.htm**.

VOLCANO WORLD ➤ *p. 209*

This Volcano World web site at **http://volcano.und.nodak.edu/** tells you everything you want to know (and a lot you don't!) about volcanos.

KIDS' SPACE ➤ *p. 210*

The Kids' Space web site at **http://www.interport.net/kids-space/** provides a way for children from different cultures to meet each other safely on the Internet.

THE EXPLORATORIUM ➤ *p. 211*

The Exploratorium museum web site at **http://www.exploratorium.edu** in San Francisco includes online exhibits exploring science, art, and human perception.

With all the talk about Internet pornography and online predators, you might think that the Web isn't a good place for kids. But nothing could be farther from the truth. The Web provides scads of neat sites for kids and parents. This chapter identifies ten of the best.

CYBERKIDS

http://www.cyberkids.com/index.html

CyberKids (see Figure 14.1) is a fun, colorful magazine for children. You go to the issue you want, and the table of contents shows you top-notch articles, stories, poems, and artwork by children, as well as product reviews and the occasional recipe.

Figure 14.1 CyberKids is an online magazine for children

There are CyberKids web site links to a similar web site for teenagers, the CyberTeens page.

The neat thing about the CyberKids pages is that they let children interact. Children submit stories, poems, artwork, and even compositions, and they help judge contests. They can also find e-mail "pen pals" through the Comments section of the home page. Kids can play a game, too—CyberKids only has Concentration, but it plans to offer more games.

PARENTSPLACE

http://www.parentsplace.com/readroom/ health.html

ParentsPlace (see Figure 14.2) provides good information on basic and preventative health care for children, including information about what to put in a first-aid kit for your child and how to treat fevers. It also has links to other health care information and vaccination information on the

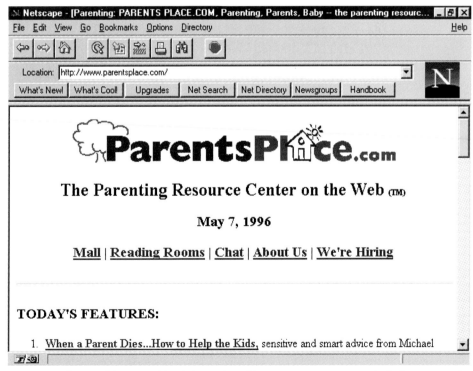

Figure 14.2 ParentsPlace provides information of interest to parents—particularly parents of small children

World Wide Web. If you have a question about your child, you can also ask the Web Doctor, a physician who answers general questions about kids' health. The questions range from what the best sleeping position for newborns is, to whether bee sting allergies are hereditary.

PARENT SOUP

http://www.parentsoup.com

The Parent Soup web site also provides reviews of good kids' sites.

Parent Soup (see Figure 14.3) supplies an enormous amount of information on parenting, in a well-designed magazine format. It has articles on how to deal with difficult—but common—questions such as how to cope with sibling rivalry, teenage alcohol problems, and money issues (like taxes). The Parent Soup online forum lets parents share information and opinions on all kinds of topics, from breast-feeding to budgeting to good books and games for kids. A lot of parents participate in the bulletin boards and chat rooms, so there's a pretty good discussion going on

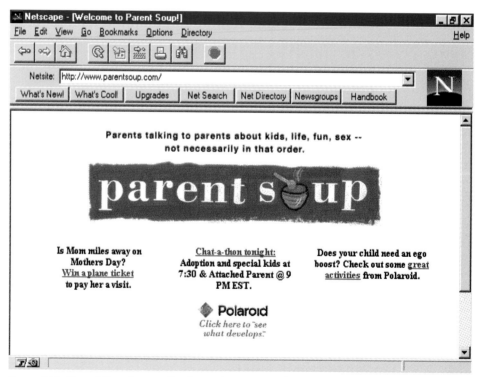

Figure 14.3 Parent Soup is an online forum for parents with children of all ages

CAUTION

This page wasn't

made for younger children.

They will need a parent

to help them sift through all

the information here.

most topics. Probably the most important thing here, for harried parents, is a series of relaxation exercises.

NATIONAL AERONAUTICS AND SPACE ADMINISTRATION

http://www.nasa.gov

Children interested in space flight or astronomy should visit the NASA web site (see Figure 14.4). The NASA web pages describe NASA's nine most recent missions, report on current or upcoming launches, and even provide live coverage of all NASA missions. This site provides answers to all of the common questions people ask about space travel, such as how astronauts go to the bathroom in space (with a special toilet that uses air rather than water to move waste), and how you can become an astronaut (you need at least a bachelor's degree in engineering, science, or mathematics and three years of related experience).

Figure 14.4 Anyone interested in space flight or astronomy should visit the NASA web site

MISTER ROGERS' NEIGHBORHOOD

http://www.pbs.org/rogers

The Mister Rogers' Neighborhood web pages (see Figure 14.5) target parents and educators, not children. These pages suggest books that relate to themes discussed on *Mister Rogers' Neighborhood*, provide lyrics to the most popular songs on the show, and describe activities that parents and teachers can plan. Some of these activities teach children to make food and objects such as sculptures and puppets. Others help children conquer their fears, express their feelings, or learn how to cooperate. And still others provide a safe way for children to express themselves and develop their imaginations by dancing, telling stories, or drawing.

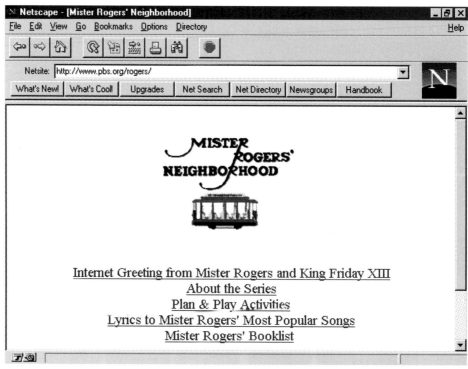

Figure 14.5 It's a beautiful day in the neighborhood, a beautiful day for a neighbor...

DISNEY

http://www.disney.com

You knew the folks at Disney would do a bang-up job, right? The Disney web site (see Figure 14.6) provides photos, audio clips, video clips, downloadable icons, and downloadable wallpaper images for many Disney movies. For some of the more popular movies, like *Pocahontas* and *Toy Story,* the web site even provides hypertext picture books that kids can enjoy.

The part of the Disney web site that delivers the most fun for children, though, is the Fun And Games section. These pages provide pictures from Disney movies that children can print and color, trivia quizzes about Disney movies, a *Toy Story* concentration/matching game, and best of all, ten experiments from *Bill Nye the Science Guy* that kids can try at home.

Figure 14.6 Preschool and early elementary age children will love the Disney web site

KID SAFETY ON THE INTERNET

http://www.uoknor.edu/oupd/kidsafe/start.htm

The University of Oklahoma Department of Public Safety created this fun, easy set of pages for children to browse through to learn basic safety information. The web pages (see Figure 14.7) cover topics such as what to do in a fire, how to be safe on the Internet, how to avoid strangers and drugs, and how to get help if you're lost. The page really takes advantage of hypertext: children navigate from page to page by clicking on buttons and arrows. Each page supplies a little bit of textual information and a picture to illustrate the points, so it's interesting and hopefully children will keep reading.

Figure 14.7 Perfect for elementary age children (and their parents!), the Kid Safety on the Internet web site teaches personal safety

VOLCANO WORLD

http://volcano.und.nodak.edu/

This page (see Figure 14.8) really has everything you wanted to know (and a lot you didn't!) about volcanos. It's pretty easy to navigate, but it's not specifically for kids, so parents should probably help younger children find their way around. On this page, you can look at pictures and videos of volcanos erupting now, older volcanos, and even volcanos on Mars and the Moon. You can also learn about volcanos in general or about specific volcanos, and you can ask a volcanologist questions. For children, the page offers fun online and hypertext lessons. The page also has a mall, where you can buy volcano-related products, and hyperlinks to more volcano information.

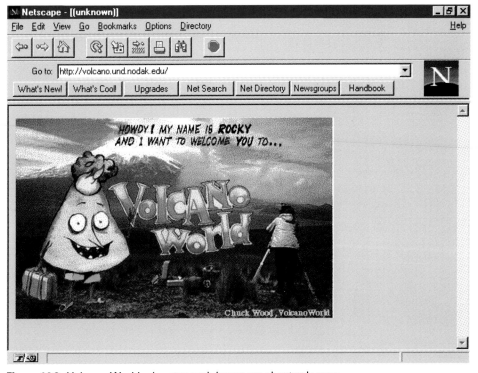

Figure 14.8 Volcano World educates web browsers about volcanos

KIDS' SPACE

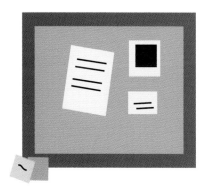

http://www.interport.net/kids-space/

The Kids' Space page (see Figure 14.9) provides a way for children from different cultures to safely meet each other on the Internet. It has a pen-pal box for children to become "pen pals," a small bulletin board, and a place for children to put their home pages up on the World Wide Web. It also publishes stories and pictures that children submit, and may soon publish audio clips as well. So far, children from more than 60 countries are using the page. Volunteers monitor everything put up on this page, so you don't have to worry about your children seeing offensive stories or messages on the page.

Figure 14.9 Using the Kids' Space web site, your son or daughter can find an international pen pal

THE EXPLORATORIUM

http://www.exploratorium.edu

The Exploratorium museum in San Francisco created this web site (see Figure 14.10) dedicated to science, art, and human perception. Children can look at electronic versions of Exploratorium exhibits. In one of these exhibits, a voice reads the story of "Ladle Rat Rotten Hut," a version of "Little Red Riding Hood" with the intonations of the words changed. Another exhibit shows mutant fruit flies. The page also has a "Science Snackbook," a series of experiments children can build by themselves, such as an experiment that uses a hair dryer to suspend a small ball in the air.

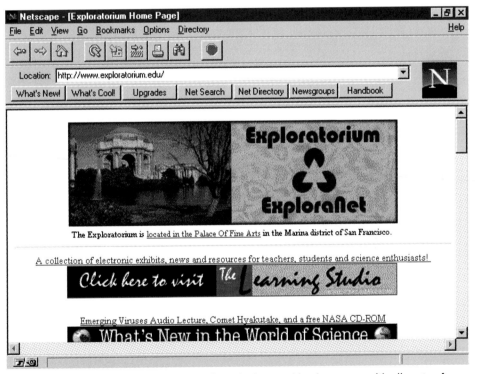

Figure 14.10 The Exploratorium museum's web site provides browsers with all sorts of wacky fun

ON FROM HERE

That was it! There is no more (at least if you've read the preceding chapters). Since I have a compulsive personality, however, I just want to remind you that this book also provides three appendixes: Appendix A explains how to connect to the Internet and install your browser. Appendix B briefly describes how you use the Microsoft Internet Explorer web browser. (In this book, I emphasize the more popular Netscape Navigator web browser.) Finally, Appendix C describes some stuff of interest to Apple Macintosh users.

APPENDIX

A

Installing Your Web Browser

Installing your web browser requires that you take three steps: You need to pick an Internet service provider. You need to acquire the web browser and Internet connection software. (Curiously, this is the hardest part.) And you need to install the web browser software.

Some of the Internet service providers give you unlimited access to the Internet and the World Wide Web for about $20 a month. The online services start charging you extra once you connect for more than a specified number of hours a month.

PICKING AN INTERNET SERVICE PROVIDER

Your first installation step is simple. You need to pick an Internet service provider. My suggestion is that you pick one of the big online services that provide Internet access and a bunch of other stuff as well: America Online (the biggest), CompuServe (the oldest), or Microsoft Network (the newest). An online service recruits subscribers who pay to view information and use services provided by the online service, but online services provide as one of their services access to the Internet. I don't think it matters all that much which service you choose, by the way. Flip a coin.

Diehard Internet junkies won't agree with this advice, by the way. They will suggest you sign up with some little mom-and-pop Internet service provider because, well, just because. An Internet service provider only does one thing: provide Internet connections. Nevertheless, I urge you to sign up with one of the big companies. You'll encounter fewer problems because you'll be following in the footsteps of the millions who have gone before you. You'll get better customer service if you do have problems. You'll get access to a bunch of additional content that nobody but other subscribers will get to see. And you'll probably get to connect to the Internet while you're on the road for the price of a local telephone call.

GETTING THE SOFTWARE YOU NEED

This is the hard part—for a stupid reason, really. Some of the companies that provide the software you need (including Microsoft Corporation and Netscape Communications Corporation) want you to acquire their software electronically. And this probably sounded easy enough to the young MBA, Reynolds, who thought up the idea. I imagine that Reynolds figured it would be really neat if the company could just use the Internet to distribute the software because, as Reynolds probably said, "Hey, remember, this is the Internet we're talking about!" The thing is—and you would think they teach this at the better business schools—people need an Internet connection first in order for this approach to work.

The first suggestion I have, therefore, is that you forget the electronic distribution gimmick. Get a real software distribution kit—in other words, a box with floppy disks or a CD.

If you've chosen to use America Online or CompuServe, you can get this kit simply by telephoning. Call America Online at 1-800-827-6364 or CompuServe at 1-800-368-3343. Tell them you want to subscribe to their service. Tell them you want to be able to browse the World Wide Web. They'll send you the software you need for free (or a small charge).

If you want to use the Microsoft Network, you'll need to get Microsoft's Internet Starter Kit. Unfortunately, you can't get one of these for-free kits by calling. (Remember the story of Reynolds?) But you can get a kit. I saw one at a computer retail store last week for around $20. A software mail order place advertised one for $10 in a flyer I got yesterday. If you want to save a trip to the store and don't yet have a favorite direct-mail place, call Egghead Software at 1-800-EGGHEAD.

If you don't want to use an online service as your Internet service provider, or you want to pick your own web browser and Internet connection software—such as Netscape's—get Netscape's Internet Starter Kit. You can get this directly from Netscape (call 1-415-528-2555), from a computer retail store, or from a direct-mail place. You'll pay quite a bit more. Maybe $50 or so. I don't think it's worth it to pay $50 for one web browser when you can get another one for free or almost free. But it's your money.

INSTALLING YOUR WEB BROWSER SOFTWARE

Unfortunately, it's really difficult for me to give precise instructions for installing your web browser software. This is true for two reasons. I don't know which Internet service provider you've selected. And I don't know which web browser you've chosen. Nevertheless, I can give you some general instructions.

Installing a Browser Under Windows 95

None of the browser software is difficult to install under Windows 95. To install a web browser (and any related software), insert the floppy disk or CD with the browser program on it into your PC's floppy drive or CD drive. Then follow these steps:

1. Click the Start button.
2. Choose the Settings Control Panel command so that Windows 95 displays the Control Panel window (see Figure A.1).
3. Double-click the Add/Remove Programs icon. Then follow the onscreen instructions.

Figure A.1 The Control Panel's Add/Remove Programs tool lets you easily install new programs

Installing a Web Browser Under Windows 3.1

I don't want to sound flip, but the right way to install a web browser on a PC that's running Windows 3.1 is to first upgrade to Windows 95 and then to follow the instructions I just provided. Windows 95 should cost you about $80 or so (if you're upgrading). But it'll make browsing the Web much, much easier. You'll also be able to retrieve web pages much, much faster.

If for some reason upgrading to Windows 95 isn't an option, make sure that you get a Windows 3.1 version of a web browser program and, if you're connecting to an online service, of whatever other software you need. Then start Windows and follow these steps:

1. Insert the CD or floppy disk with the web browser software on it into either your CD drive or floppy drive.
2. Display the Program Manager window.
3. Choose the File|Run command.
4. When Program Manager displays the Run dialog box, enter the command for starting the installation program. Typically you'll enter the drive letter of the CD drive or floppy drive from which you're installing the software, a colon (:), and then the name of the installation program. If you're installing the web browser software from your A floppy drive and the installation program is named "install," for example, you enter **a:install** into the Run dialog box's only text box. If you're installing the web browser software from your D CD drive and the installation program is named "setup," you enter **d:setup** into the Run dialog box's only text box.

Installing a Web Browser on an Apple Mac

As you knew it would be, installing a web browser on a Mac is easiest. (That's one of the reasons you bought the thing, right?) You can probably guess how this works, but my compulsive personality requires I tell you the steps (see Figure A.2):

1. Insert the floppy disk or CD from the software distribution kit into the appropriate drive of your Mac.
2. Double-click on the floppy disk or CD's icon once it appears on the desktop.
3. Double-click on the Installer icon and follow the onscreen instructions.

CAUTION

You may need to update elements of the Macintosh operating system in order to run Netscape. The Netscape software distribution kit, however, comes with the new stuff you need. Look in the System Updates folder.

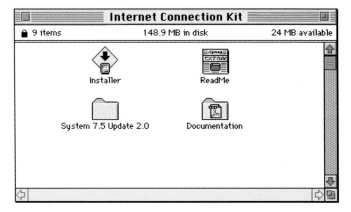

Figure A.2 After you double-click the floppy disk or CD's desktop icon, your Mac opens a window showing what's on the disk

Using Microsoft's Internet Explorer

The previous chapters of this book assume you're using Netscape's Navigator to browse the Web, but Netscape isn't the only web browser. Microsoft Corporation sells another web browser called Internet Explorer, which is very good and has several advantages over Netscape: it's cheaper (and sometimes even free), it's faster, and it's easy to start and use (especially for new users). For these reasons, I want to quickly describe how to use the Internet Explorer. Once you know how the Internet Explorer works—and it works very similarly to Netscape—you can easily use this book, even though it emphasizes the Netscape way.

STARTING INTERNET EXPLORER

When you install the Internet Explorer—something you do by running the Windows 95 Internet Setup Wizard—the setup program automatically adds an Internet Explorer shortcut icon to the Windows 95 desktop. To start the Internet Explorer, you double-click the Internet Explorer icon. If you're using the Microsoft Network as your Internet service provider, you next see the Microsoft Network logon screen. You click Connect. A few seconds later, the Internet Explorer program window appears and loads your first web page, called a *home page* (see Figure B.1).

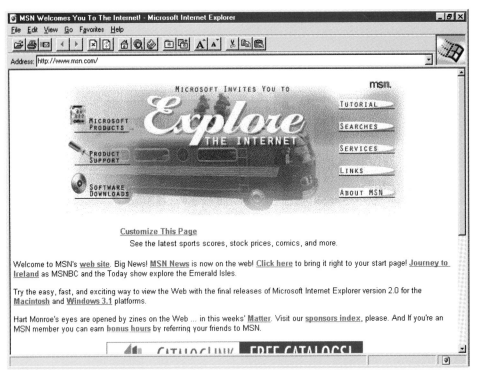

Figure B.1 The first page your web browser displays is called a home page

USING HYPERLINKS TO MOVE BETWEEN WEB PAGES

Internet Explorer changes the mouse pointer to a hand with an extended pointer finger whenever you point to a hyperlink.

As with any web browser, you move between web pages by clicking hyperlinks with your mouse. By clicking on a hyperlink—which can be a chunk of text or a picture—you tell the web browser to move you to another web page. For example, if you click on the Software Downloads hyperlink,

your web browser displays the web page shown in Figure B.2.

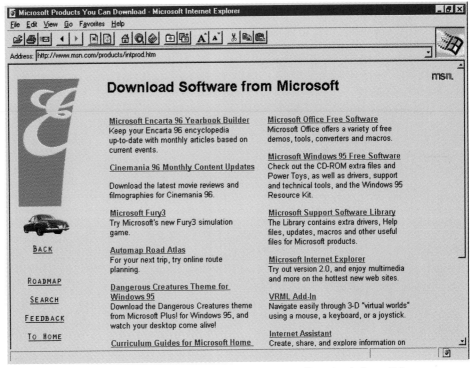

Figure B.2 Here's what you see after you click the Software Downloads hyperlink

One thing that can be a little tricky about hyperlinks, however, is that they don't always stand out on a web page. In Figure B.1, for example, things are pretty clear. You can probably guess that the icons and tabs at the top of the web page are clickable—and therefore are hyperlinks. But take a close look at Figure B.2. Or better yet, take a close look at your screen if you're following along in front of your computer. You'll notice that some of the text appears in a different color if you're working along. These colored chunks of text also represent hyperlinks. So if you click Microsoft Fury3

Microsoft Fury3
Try Microsoft's new Fury3 simulation game.

your web browser displays the web page shown in Figure B.3.

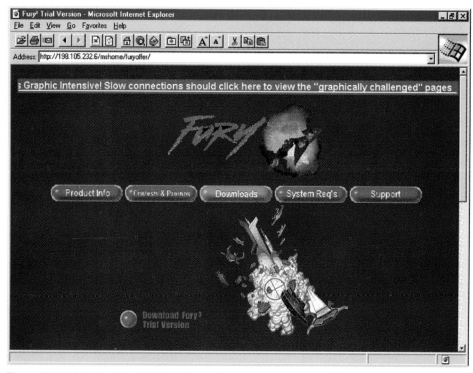

Figure B.3 This is the Fury Trial Version web page

By the way, you've now learned a dirty little secret of the Internet and, in particular, the World Wide Web. It's slow. Even if you've got a superfast modem, you'll spend most of your time waiting for some distant web server to transmit the web page you've requested by clicking a hyperlink. But don't be discouraged. What you need to do is minimize the time you spend waiting for useless information. The chapters of this book should help you do just that.

PAGING TO THE PREVIOUS OR NEXT WEB PAGE

You can page back and forth to the web pages you've already viewed by clicking the Previous and Next buttons.

You don't need to wait until your browser finishes retrieving a web page before you click a new hyperlink or you page back and forth. You can stop retrieving one page and move to another page at any time.

One thing you'll notice if you do this (and go ahead and try it right now) is that redisplaying a page you've already viewed takes only a split second.

You can quickly redisplay web pages you've recently viewed because your web browser actually stores, or *caches,* a copy of the web page on your computer's hard disk. So when you redisplay a web page, your web browser only has to go to the work of grabbing the file from your hard disk—a very fast operation—rather than grabbing the file from some distant web server.

If you want your web browser to grab a new copy of a web page rather than one from its cache, you click the Refresh button.

You might want to do this, for example, if a web page displays information that is frequently updated: web pages linked to cameras that continually take new pictures, weather maps updated based on new satellite data, and so forth.

If a web page is taking too long to load, you can always tell Internet Explorer to give up. To do this, click the Stop button.

CREATING AND USING FAVORITE PLACES

Other web browsers use different names for these memorized pages. Netscape, for example, calls them bookmarks.

In Chapter 3, I discuss in detail the painfully cryptic addresses—called *URLs*—that the Internet uses to identify the precise locations of web sites and their web pages. You'll soon enough learn how to work with these URLs, but even when you do, you'll still find it really useful to have your browser memorize often-visited web page addresses. Internet Explorer calls these memorized addresses *Favorites*.

To tell Internet Explorer it should memorize the current web server or web page address, choose the Add To Favorites tool.

To later view a web page you've marked as a favorite, choose the Open Favorites tool.

When Internet Explorer displays the Favorites dialog box (see Figure B.4), choose the web page you want to view.

SAVING CONTENT

You can usually save the information shown in the browser window. This means that if a web page shows a picture, you can save the picture. And if a web page has a bunch of textual information—maybe it's an article on retirement planning—you can save that, too.

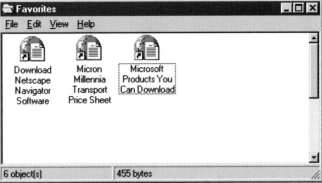

Figure B.4 The Favorites dialog box shows all of the favorite web pages you've asked Internet Explorer to memorize

CAUTION

As noted elsewhere in this book, web page designs change often. So don't expect the web pages shown in this appendix to match what you see on your screen. Almost surely by the time you view them, the web pages I'm describing will have changed.

Saving the Textual Portion of a Web Page

To save the textual portion of a web page, choose the File|Save As command. When Internet Explorer displays the Save As dialog box (see Figure B.5), use the Save In box to specify where Internet Explorer should save a file that contains the textual portion of the web page. Use the Save As Type box to specify that you just want "plain text" saved. Then use the File Name box to name the text file you're creating. When you finish all this, click Save.

Figure B.5 Use the Save As dialog box to name the file and specify where on your hard disk it should be stored

Saving Graphic Images

To save a graphic image shown in a web page, right-click the image so that Internet Explorer displays its shortcut menu (see Figure B.6).

Then choose the Save Picture As command; Internet Explorer displays the Save As dialog box. Use the Save In box to specify where Internet Explorer should save the graphic image file. Use the File Name box to name the file. Then click Save.

Downloading Files

Some hyperlinks don't point to other web pages. They point to downloadable files. When you click one of these hyperlinks, what you're really telling Internet Explorer to do is retrieve, or *download,* the file from the web server or even another type of server such as an FTP server. I talk about FTP and its special servers in Chapter 6.

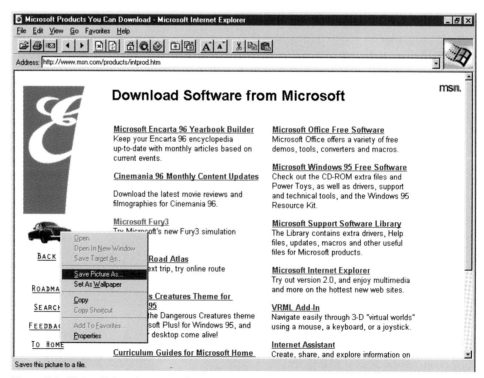

Figure B.6 Right-click an image to display a shortcut menu with the command you use to save the image

FORMS WORK LIKE DIALOG BOXES

You need to know about just one other topic to easily work with the Web: how to use forms. *Forms* are just web pages that include check boxes and option buttons you mark, text boxes you fill in, and command buttons you click. You use forms to order products, play interactive games, register for online services, and enter data for web calculators and search services.

Rather than take the time to load a web page that uses each of these form elements, however, let's just take a look at an Internet Explorer dialog box that uses each of these elements. Choose the View|Options command. When Internet Explorer displays the Options dialog box, click the Advanced tab to display its page of option settings (see Figure B.7). (By the way, don't worry about any of these settings.

If you know how to work with the dialog boxes that get displayed when you choose some commands, you know how to work with forms.

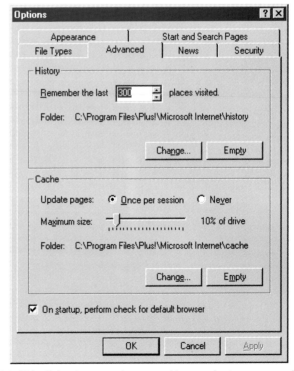

Some text boxes, like the one shown in Figure B.7, let you adjust the value using buttons.

Figure B.7 This dialog box uses boxes and buttons just as some web page forms do

231

Just focus on the mechanics of using the buttons and boxes that the dialog box displays.)

Along the top edge of the dialog box is a text box called Remember The Last Places Visited. The text box element is common to both dialog boxes and web page forms. In essence, a *text box* is simply an input blank you fill in with some bit of information. To enter data into a text box, click the box and then begin typing. To replace the contents of a text box, double-click it and then type the new entry.

Another element common to both dialog boxes and web page forms is *command buttons.* You click command buttons to tell Internet Explorer to accept the information you've provided by clicking buttons and filling in boxes on a form. The dialog box in Figure B.7, for example, has two sets of Change and Empty command buttons, and then along the bottom edge, the OK, Cancel, and Apply command buttons. Web page forms don't usually have these command buttons, but you'll often see another command button named something like "Submit," "Search," or "Send." Clicking one of these buttons tells your web browser to send the information you've collected with the form to the web server so it can process the information in some way.

I describe what a cache is and how you use it in the final section of this appendix.

Another element you'll commonly see on dialog boxes and forms is *option buttons*—such as the Update Pages option buttons—Once Per Session and Never—shown in the Cache settings part of the Advanced tab. Option buttons represent mutually exclusive choices. You mark your choice by clicking the button. When you click the button, Internet Explorer places a dot, or *bullet,* in the center of the button to show you've selected it.

Let me mention one final element you'll see on both dialog boxes and forms: a check box. *Check boxes* are, in effect, on-off buttons. If the check box is marked, Internet Explorer places a check mark or an *X* in the box. To mark and unmark a check box, you click the box with your mouse. You can see an example check box at the bottom of the Advanced tab, a box labeled "On Startup, Perform Check For Default Browser."

TWEAKING AND TROUBLESHOOTING INTERNET EXPLORER

Chapter 10 describes adjustments you can make so the Netscape web browser runs more smoothly and techniques you can use to fix problems you encounter. Much of the information provided in that chapter also applies to Internet Explorer (so you'll want to read Chapter 10). In a handful of cases, however, the actual mechanics of fine-tuning Internet Explorer (as compared to Netscape) differ slightly. For this reason, I want to quickly talk about how you change your home (start) page, browse only the textual information on web pages, and change the way Internet Explorer caches.

Changing Your Home Page

Internet Explorer initially uses the **http://home.msn.com** URL as your home, or start, page. Unless you're really spending time reading that page every single time you start Internet Explorer, however, you should change your home page. If there's some other page you want to always or almost always view, for example, you may make that your home page. (Make sure that whatever web page you choose as your home page is one that usually is accessible.) To make this change, first display the web page that you want to see whenever you start Internet Explorer. Then choose the View|Options command, click the Start And Search Pages tab, and click the Use Current command button (see Figure B.8).

Viewing Web Page Text

You can change the way that Internet Explorer runs in order to improve the speed with which you browse web pages. Perhaps the easiest thing to do—and I usually work this way—is *not* to load the graphical images that pepper most pages. This probably makes sense

habits & strategies

If you almost always start your web browsing using a search service, use the search service's form as your home page. Chapter 5 describes how to use a search service.

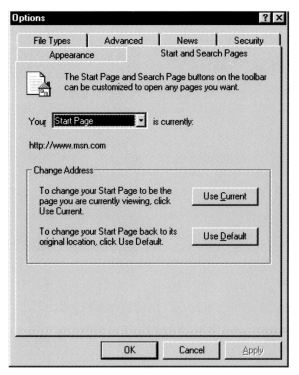

Figure B.8 You can use the Start And Search Page tab of the Options dialog box to change the home page that Internet Explorer automatically loads every time you start it

to you. It might be typical to have a 50K web page with 90 percent of its content represented by graphical images and only 10 percent of its content represented by the text you're reading. Thus, 90 percent of the time, you're sitting there twiddling your thumbs while the graphical content downloads. Sometimes, however, it's that graphical content you want to view. And in this situation, of course, you want to take the time to grab this information. Other times, however, the graphical content is only fluff—simply frosting on the cake. And in those situations, it makes sense to tell Internet Explorer to grab only the textual information.

To do this, choose the View|Options command, click the Appearance tab, and then unmark the Show Pictures, Play Sounds, and Show

Animations check boxes. From this point on, Internet Explorer won't automatically load the graphical content of a page, play sounds, or show animation. It will only display text. If you want to see a picture or animation, or play a sound, you can click the icon that Internet Explorer displays in place of the picture, animation, or sound.

Adjusting the Web Page Cache

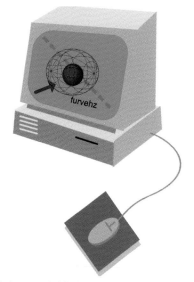

There's one final adjustment you can make to improve the speed with which Internet Explorer displays web pages. You can increase the size of the cache. This sounds complicated, I know, but let me explain. If you repeatedly view some web pages—and the web pages don't change between viewing—you actually end up retrieving the same web page information multiple times. And that's silly because repeatedly moving that same 50K document from some distant web site to your computer is time-consuming. What you should do—and this is probably obvious now—is hang on to a copy of the web page by storing it someplace on your computer. Then you can grab this copy from your hard disk (which Internet Explorer can do very quickly), rather than grabbing the web page from its usual web site.

This technique is called *caching.* Internet Explorer is already set up to cache, but you can adjust (and possibly improve) the way it works. To do this, choose the View|Options command and click the Advanced tab (see Figure B.9). Then use the History and Cache settings to fine-tune the cache. For example, you can increase the number of web pages cached by increasing the value in the Remember Last Places Visited text box. If you need to make more room to cache all those pages, you can adjust the Maximum Size slider button upward. You can

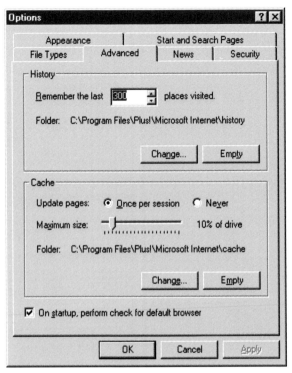

Figure B.9 The Advanced tab of the Options dialog box lets you control the way Internet Explorer's caching works

also use the Update Pages option to specify whether Internet Explorer retrieves updated copies of a web page from the original web site once per session or never at all.

Using Netscape on an Apple Macintosh

This book emphasizes the PC way of doing things. If you're a Mac user, you probably feel a little shortchanged. I didn't forget you, however. This appendix quickly describes how you use the Netscape Navigator on an Apple Macintosh. Once you know the basics, you can easily use this book. One other thing: although we use IBM-compatible PCs at my office, I use an Apple Macintosh at home. And I love it.

STARTING NETSCAPE ON THE MAC

When you install Netscape on the Mac, it adds another folder to the Launcher called Internet Kit. Display this Launcher folder. Click the Apple Internet Dialer icon to connect to the Internet and sign up with an Internet service. Once you have done this, click the Netscape Navigator icon to start the Netscape web browser. A few seconds later, the Netscape program window appears and loads your first web page, called a *home page* (see Figure C.1).

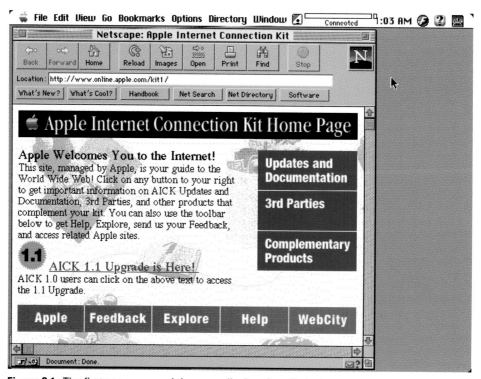

Figure C.1 The first page your web browser displays is called a home page

The first time you click the Apple Internet Dialer's icon, you register for an Internet service provider. This isn't difficult. Just follow the onscreen instructions. And have your credit card ready.

USING HYPERLINKS TO MOVE BETWEEN WEB PAGES

As with any web browser, you move between web pages by clicking hyperlinks with your mouse. By clicking on a hyperlink—which can be a chunk of text or a picture—you tell the web browser to move you to another web page. For example, if you click on the Updates And Documentation button

Updates and Documentation

your web browser displays the web page shown in Figure C.2.

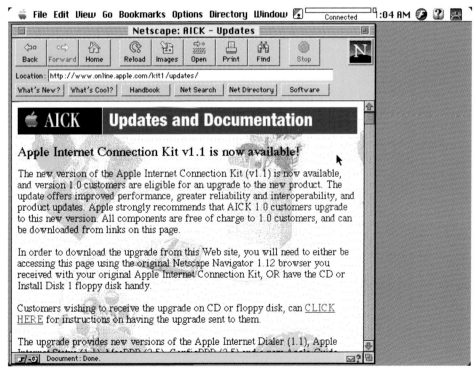

Figure C.2 Here's what you see after you click the Updates And Documentation button

Netscape changes the mouse pointer to a hand with an extended pointer finger whenever you point to a hyperlink.

One thing that can be a little tricky about hyperlinks, however, is that they don't always stand out on a web page. In Figure C.1, for example, things are pretty clear. You can probably guess that the rows of buttons at the bottom of the web page and along the right edge are clickable—and therefore hyperlinks. But take a close look at Figure C.2. Or better yet, take a close look at your screen if you're following along in front of your computer. You'll notice that some of the text appears in a different color if you're working along. These colored chunks of text also represent hyperlinks.

By the way, you've now learned a dirty little secret of the Internet and, in particular, the World Wide Web. It's slow. Even if you've got a superfast modem, you'll spend most of your time waiting for some distant web server to transmit the web page you've requested by clicking a hyperlink. But don't be discouraged. What you need to do is minimize the time you spend waiting for useless information. The chapters of this book should help you do just that.

PAGING TO THE PREVIOUS OR NEXT WEB PAGE

You can page back and forth to the web pages you've already viewed by clicking the Back and Forward buttons (see Figure C.2). One thing you'll notice if you do this (and go ahead and try it right now) is that redisplaying a page you've already viewed takes only a split second.

You can quickly redisplay web pages you've recently viewed because your web browser actually stores, or *caches,* a copy of the web page on your computer's hard disk. So when you redisplay a web page, your web browser only has to go to the work of grabbing the file from your hard disk—a very fast operation—rather than grabbing the file from some distant web server.

If you want your web browser to grab a new copy of a web page rather than one from its cache, you click the Reload button (see Figure C.2). You might want to do this, for example, if a web page displays

habits & strategies

You don't need to wait until your browser finishes retrieving a web page before you click a new hyperlink or you page back and forth. You can stop retrieving one page and move to another page at any time.

CAUTION

information that is frequently updated: web pages linked to cameras that continually take new pictures, weather maps updated based on new satellite data, and so forth.

If some web page is taking too long to load, you can always tell Netscape to give up. To do this, click the Stop button.

CREATING AND USING FAVORITE PLACES

In Chapter 3, I discuss in detail the painfully cryptic addresses—called *URLs*—that the Internet uses to identify the precise locations of web sites and their web pages. You'll soon enough learn how to work with these URLs, but even when you do, you'll still find it really useful to have your browser memorize often-visited web page addresses. Netscape calls these memorized addresses, *bookmarks.* To tell Netscape it should memorize the current web server or web page address, choose the Bookmarks|Add Bookmarks command. To later view a web page you've marked as a favorite, activate the Bookmarks menu, and then choose the bookmarked web page you want to view.

SAVING CONTENT

You can usually save the information shown in the browser window. This means that if a web page shows a picture, you can save the picture. And if a web page has a bunch of textual information—maybe it's an article on moving to the south of France—you can save that, too.

Saving the Textual Portion of a Web Page

To save the textual portion of a web page, choose the File|Save As command. When Netscape displays the Save As dialog box (see Figure C.3), use the list boxes to specify where Netscape should save a file that contains the textual portion of the web page. Use the Format box to specify that you just want "plain text" saved. Then use the Save As box to name the text file you're creating. When you finish all this, click Save.

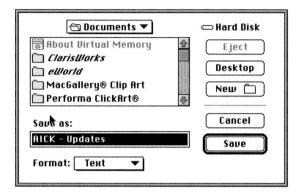

Figure C.3 Use the Save As dialog box to name the file and specify where on your hard disk it should be stored

Saving Graphic Images

To save a graphic image shown in a web page, choose the File|Save As command. When Netscape displays the Save As dialog box (see Figure C.3), use the list boxes to specify where Netscape should save the file. Use the Format box to specify that you just want the file saved in its "source" format. Then use the Save As box to name the file. When you finish all this, click Save.

Downloading Files

Some hyperlinks don't point to other web pages. They point to files. When you click one of these hyperlinks, what you're really telling Netscape to do is to retrieve, or *download,* the file from the web server or even another type of server such as an FTP server. I talk about FTP and its special servers in Chapter 6.

FORMS WORK LIKE DIALOG BOXES

You need to know about just one other topic to easily work with the Web: how to use forms. Fortunately, if you've been working with your Mac for more than about a day or two, you already know how to do this. *Forms* are just web pages that work and look like dialog boxes. They include check boxes and option buttons you mark, text boxes you fill in, and command buttons you click. You use forms to order products, play interactive games, register for online services, and enter data for web calculators and search services.

TWEAKING AND TROUBLESHOOTING NETSCAPE

Chapter 10 describes adjustments you can make so the Netscape web browser runs more smoothly and techniques you can use to fix problems you encounter. Much of the information provided in that chapter also applies to Netscape on the Mac (so you'll want to read Chapter 10). Nevertheless, some of the mechanics work slightly different on a Mac. So let me close this appendix by talking about these differences.

Changing Your Home Page

Netscape initially uses the **http://home.online.apple.com/kit1** URL as your home (start) page. Unless you're really spending time reading that page every single time you start Netscape, however, you should change your home page. If there's some other page you want to always or almost always view, for example, you may make that your home page. (Make sure that whatever web page you choose as your home page is one that usually is accessible.) To make this change, start Netscape and choose the Options|General Preferences command. Netscape displays the Preferences: General dialog box (see Figure C.4).

Viewing Web Page Text

You can change the way that Netscape runs in order to improve the speed with which you browse web pages. Perhaps the easiest thing to do—and I usually work this way—is *not* to load the graphical images that pepper most pages. This probably makes sense to you. It might be typical to have a 50K web page with 90 percent of its content represented by graphical images and only 10 percent of its content represented by the text you're reading. Thus, 90 percent of the time, you're sitting there twiddling your thumbs while graphical content downloads. Sometimes, it's that graphical content you want to view. And in this situation, of course, you want to take the time to grab this

habits & strategies

If you almost always start your web browsing using a search service, use the search service's form as your home page. Chapter 4 describes how to use a search service.

Preferences: General

| Appearance | Colors | Fonts | Helpers | Images | Applications | Languages |

Toolbars

Show Toolbar as: ○ Pictures   ○ Text   ● Pictures and Text

Startup

On Startup Launch: ● Netscape Browser   ○ Netscape Mail   ○ Netscape News

Browser starts with:

○ Blank Page
● Home Page Location: http://www.online.apple.com/kit1/

Link Styles

Links are: ☒ Underlined
Followed Links Expire: ○ Never ● After 30 days   Now

Cancel   Apply   OK

Figure C.4 Use the Preferences: General dialog box to fine-tune the way Netscape works

information. Other times, however, the graphical content is only fluff—simply frosting on the cake. And in those situations, it makes sense to tell Netscape to grab only the textual information.

To do this, choose the Options|Autoload Images command. This turns off the automatic loading of images, and Netscape removes the checkmark from the command. From this point on, Netscape won't automatically load the graphical content of a page. It will only display text. If you want to see the pictures on a page, click the Images icon. If you want to turn the automatic loading of images back on, choose the command again, and Netscape adds a checkmark in front of the command name.

Adjusting the Web Page Cache

There's one final adjustment you can make to improve the speed with which Netscape displays web pages. You can increase the size of the cache. This sounds complicated, I know, but let me explain. If you repeatedly view some web pages—and the web pages don't change between viewing—you actually end up retrieving the same web page information multiple times. And that's silly because repeatedly moving that same 50K document from some distant web site to your computer is time-consuming. What you should do—and this is probably obvious now—is hang on to a copy of the web page by storing it someplace on your computer. Then you can grab this copy from your hard disk (which Netscape can do very quickly), rather than grabbing the web page from its usual web site.

This technique is called *caching*. Netscape is already set up to cache, but you can adjust (and possibly improve) the way it works. To do this, choose the Options|Network Preferences command so Netscape displays the Preferences: Network dialog box (see Figure C.5). Then use the Cache settings to fine-tune the cache. For example, you can increase the number of web pages cached by increasing the Cache Size value. You can also use the Check Documents buttons to specify how often Netscape retrieves updated copies of a web page from the original web site.

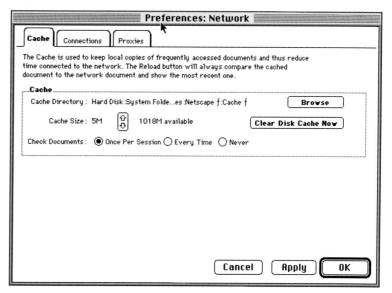

Figure C.5 The Preferences: Network dialog box lets you control the way Netscape's caching works

Index

Note: Page numbers in *italics* refer to illustrations.

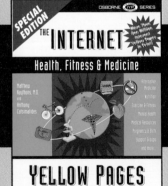

DIGITAL DESIGN FOR THE 21ST CENTURY

You can count on Osborne/McGraw-Hill and its expert authors to bring you the inside scoop on digital design, production, and the best-selling graphics software.

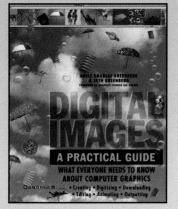

Digital Images: A Practical Guide
by Adele Droblas Greenberg
and Seth Greenberg
$26.95 U.S.A., ISBN 0-07-882113-4

Scanning the Professional Way
by Sybil Ihrig and Emil Ihrig
$21.95 U.S.A., ISBN 0-07-882145-2

Preparing Digital Images for Print
by Sybil Ihrig and Emil Ihrig
$21.95 U.S.A., ISBN 0-07-882146-0

**Fundamental Photoshop:
A Complete Introduction,
Second Edition**
by Adele Droblas Greenberg and Seth Greenberg
$29.95 U.S.A., ISBN 0-07-882093-6

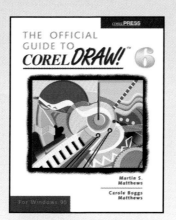

**The Official Guide to
CorelDRAW!™6 for Windows 95**
by Martin S. Matthews and Carole Boggs Matthews
$34.95 U.S.A., ISBN 0-07-882168-1

**The Official Guide to Corel
PHOTO-PAINT 6**
by David Huss
$34.95 U.S.A., ISBN 0-07-882207-6

ORDER BOOKS DIRECTLY FROM OSBORNE/McGRAW-HILL

For a complete catalog of Osborne's books, call 510-549-6600 or write to us at 2600 Tenth Street, Berkeley, CA 94710

☎ **Call Toll-Free,** *24 hours a day, 7 days a week, in the U.S.A.*
U.S.A.: 1-800-262-4729   **Canada: 1-800-565-5758**

✉ **Mail** *in the U.S.A. to:*
McGraw-Hill, Inc.
Customer Service Dept.
P.O. Box 182607
Columbus, OH 43218-2607

Canada
McGraw-Hill Ryerson
Customer Service
300 Water Street
Whitby, Ontario L1N 9B6

🖨 **Fax** *in the U.S.A. to:*
1-614-759-3644

Canada
1-800-463-5885
Canada
orders@mcgrawhill.ca

SHIP TO:

Name _____

Company _____

Address _____

City / State / Zip _____

Daytime Telephone *(We'll contact you if there's a question about your order.)*

ISBN #	BOOK TITLE	Quantity	Price	Total
0-07-88				
0-07-88				
0-07-88				
0-07-88				
0-07-88				
0-07088				
0-07-88				
0-07-88				
0-07-88				
0-07-88				
0-07-88				
0-07-88				
0-07-88				
0-07-88				

Shipping & Handling Charge from Chart Below	
Subtotal	
Please Add Applicable State & Local Sales Tax	
TOTAL	

Shipping & Handling Charges

Order Amount	U.S.	Outside U.S.
$15.00 - $24.99	$4.00	$6.00
$25.00 - $49.99	$5.00	$7.00
$50.00 - $74.99	$6.00	$8.00
$75.00 - and up	$7.00	$9.00
$100.00 - and up	$8.00	$10.00

Occasionally we allow other selected companies to use our mailing list. If you would prefer that we not include you in these extra mailings, please check here: ❏

METHOD OF PAYMENT

❏ Check or money order enclosed (payable to Osborne/McGraw-Hill)

❏ **AMERICAN EXPRESS**   ❏ **DISCOVER**   ❏ **MasterCard**   ❏ **VISA**

Account No. [ ][ ][ ][ ][ ][ ][ ][ ][ ][ ][ ][ ][ ][ ][ ][ ]

Expiration Date _____

Signature _____

In a hurry? Call with your order anytime, day or night, or visit your local bookstore.

Thank you for your order   Code BC640SL